מצות אהבת ישראל

# THE MITZVAH TO
# LOVE
YOUR FELLOW AS YOURSELF

מצות אהבת ישראל

# THE MITZVAH TO
# LOVE
### YOUR FELLOW AS YOURSELF

*a chasidic discourse by*
**Rabbi Menachem Mendel Schneersohn**
זצוקללה"ה נבג"מ זי"ע
of Lubavitch
the *Tzemach Tzedek*

•

*translated by*
**Rabbi Zalman I. Posner**
**Rabbi Nissen Mangel**

*edited by*
**Rabbi Eliezer Danzinger**
**Rabbi Avraham Vaisfiche**

**KEHOT PUBLICATION SOCIETY**
770 Eastern Parkway / Brooklyn, New York 11213

THE MITZVAH TO
LOVE YOUR FELLOW AS YOURSELF

Published and Copyright © 2002
by
KEHOT PUBLICATION SOCIETY
770 Eastern Parkway / Brooklyn, New York 11213
(718) 774-4000 / Fax (718) 774-2718

**Orders:**
291 Kingston Avenue / Brooklyn, New York 11213
(718) 778-0226 / Fax (718) 778-4148
www.kehotonline.com

All rights reserved

ISBN 0-8266-0460-9

*Manufactured in the United States of America*

# CONTENTS

*preface*

7

*portrait of Rabbi Menachem Mendel*

9

*introduction*

13

*translation and commentary*

20

*hebrew notes*

35

*brief biography*

39

*important dates*

47

*published works*

53

*appendix*

57

ב״ה

# PREFACE

The forth Lubavitcher Rebbe, Rabbi Shmuel of Lubavitch once said, "What good is Chasidus and piety if the main quality—*Ahavat Yisrael*—is lacking!?"

To that end, Torah literature in general, and Chasidus in particular, is replete with examples and directives regarding this cardinal precept.

The present chasidic discourse, by the third Lubavitcher Rebbe, Rabbi Menachem Mendel, elucidates the mystical basis of the cardinal commandment to love your fellow as yourself, while translating the esoteric into practical application.

The *maamar*, originally published in *Derech Mitzvotecha*, was translated by Rabbis Zalman I. Posner and Nissen Mangel and printed in *Kuntres Ahavat Yisrael* (*Kehot*, 1976). In 1998, a newly revised edition of *Kuntres Ahavat Yisrael* was published, edited by Rabbi Eliezer Danzinger, who included a translation of Rabbi Yoel Kahan's encyclopedic article on *Ahavat Yisrael*, in *Sefer HaArachim-Chabad*—appended here.

Included as supplements are Hebrew notes by Rabbi Menachem M. Schneerson, the Lubavitcher Rebbe. Also, a brief biography of the author's life and his published works. The two appended stories are excerpts from Rabbi Elchonon Lesches's book of stories of the Tzemach Tzedek (soon to be published).

Rabbi Avraham Vaisfiche edited the present volume and contributed to the annotations. Rabbi Shmuel Marcus coordinated the project. Special thanks to Rabbi Yosef B. Friedman for his editorial guidance.

*Kehot Publication Society*

13th of Nissan, 5762

RABBI MENACHEM MENDEL SCHNEERSOHN
OF LUBAVITCH
1789—1866

Facsimile of handwritten manuscript by Rabbi Menachem Mendel

# INTRODUCTION AND SUMMARY

INTRODUCTION AND SUMMARY

Rabbi Schneur Zalman of Liadi told his son, Rabbi DovBer: My "grandfather" (the Baal Shem Tov) said that one must practice self-sacrifice for *Ahavat Yisrael*, even toward a person one has never seen.

—*Hayom Yom*

One of the fundamental principles of Chasidism is *Ahavat Yisrael*, the love for a fellow Jew. What has Chasidic philosophy uncovered in this Biblical precept? How did emphasis on this mitzvah shape the development of the Chasidic movement, and how does it explain the philosophy of the Chabad-Lubavitch movement in particular.

The Alter Rebbe, Rabbi Schneur Zalman of Liadi, founder of Chabad-Lubavitch, set the foundation to the Chasidic concept of *Ahavat Yisrael*. In his magnum opus, *Tanya*, Chapter 32, the Alter Rebbe states regarding the "direct and easy path" toward fulfilling this mitzvah:

> "...as for the soul and spirit [of fellow Jews]...they are actually all equal; they all have one father. It is because of this common root in the One G-d that all of Israel are called "brothers"—in the full sense of the word, only the bodies are distinct from each other."

With the emphasis on the spiritual—not the division caused by the physical—states Rabbi Schneur Zalman, one can actually fulfill the biblical commandment of loving your fellow as yourself.

Rabbi Schneur Zalman quotes Hillel the Elder who stated that this precept is the "entire Torah," explaining it to mean the *purpose* of the entire Torah, "for the basis and root purpose of the entire Torah is to elevate and exalt the soul high above the body, to [G-d,] the root and source of all worlds, and also to draw down the infinite light of *Ein Sof* into the Community of Israel."

In the present discourse, Rabbi Menachem Mendel of Lubavitch, grandson of Rabbi Schneur Zalman and third Chabad-Lubavitch leader, elucidates the mystical basis of this cardinal commandment, while translating the esoteric into practical application.

The Rebbe cites the kabbalistic principle of the "collective soul of the world of *Tikkun*" thereby explaining the essential unity of all souls.

When one is conscious of the collective soul and understands the integrated relationship of each soul, the separation of our physical bodies no longer causes indifference. When we connect with each other on a spiritual level we can love our fellow as we love ourselves, for in truth, we are all one soul.

### INTEGRATED SOULS

The Rebbe first introduces an enigmatic episode related in the Talmud: A would-be proselyte asked Hillel the Elder to teach him the entire Torah "on one foot." Hillel responded "What is hateful to you do not do to your neighbor. That is the entire Torah; the rest is but commentary. Now go and study."

The Rebbe asks: is it possible that our Man-G-d relationship is mere commentary? Is the entire body of 613 mitzvot merely commentary?

To explain how loving our neighbor is fundamental to all divine service, the Rebbe analyzes the kabbalistic view of souls and their impact on High.

In Lurianic thought, "All Israel comprises one complete entity within the soul of Adam." Although free of sin, it is for this reason that Rabbi Yitzchak Luria, (the holy Arizal), would remorsefully recite the *Viduy* confession, since part of the Arizal's soul had *experienced* sin, albeit in another man's body.

The *Zohar* states that Adam was created in the image of the supernal "man" of the world of *Tikkun*. Just as the ten *Sefirot* of the supernal man incorporate an aspect of each other—*chesed* contains *gevurah*, *gevurah* contains *chesed*, and so on—so too does every soul incorporate within itself an aspect of every other soul.

## THE HUMAN ANALOGY

The Rebbe uses the human body as an analogy for this idea of transcendent unity. The body consists of various parts: head, feet, hands, nails, etc., yet, because of the confluence of blood in the circulatory system each part shares in the unity of the whole. Thus, you can cure one part of the body via an injection into another part.

The Rebbe now takes the analogy one step further, and focuses on the brain, which is the center of this transcendent vitality. The brain senses acutely the pain of a wound in any particular part of the body. Similarly, Adam's soul (which is both metaphorically and literally the head of all other souls) feels the pain of each soul even after their subsequent separation. It is only our world of separation that divides us; in truth, physical borders cannot divide a soul. We are each part of a united whole. The holy Arizal experienced this unity and therefore he confessed for the sins committed by other people. This spiritual inter-connection is the basis for loving one's fellow as oneself.

## PRE-PRAYER

It is customary to verbally accept the mitzvah of loving your fellow each day before prayer. What is the connection between this specific mitzvah and prayer?

The Rebbe sees all Jews as one body with many limbs. Just as a person needs a unified and healthy body to facilitate the energy of his soul, so too the Jewish people need to be a "unified and healthy body" so as not to obstruct the divine flow of energy attainable during the prayer of *Shema*.

This unity is not only a requirement for the individual soul to receive divine grace, but allows the soul to transcend the limitations of its own individuality by ascending into the collective soul.

Conversely, states the Rebbe, when a Jew rejects another soul from his own heart through hating another Jew, he in turn becomes defective in his ability to ascend in favor before G-d. A soul's choice to separate itself from the whole (or a part thereof) causes a spiritual blemish. And G-d says: "He who has a blemish shall not approach to offer..."

## II.

**CLASSIC LOVE**

The Rebbe now examines Hillel's adage "*What is hateful to you do not do to your fellow*" and why he paraphrased this mitzvah in the negative, and uncovers a fascinating dimension in human behavior and in the mitzvah to love your fellow as yourself.

In classical Jewish thought, Hillel's dictum is explained to stress the mitzvah as it applies to action. Just as love of one's self prohibits self-harm, similarly one should cause no harm to one's fellow.

The Rebbe interprets Hillel's words to be completely encompassing of human relationships. To illustrate the power of love, the Rebbe cites the Talmud (*Shabbat* 119a) that says: "A person sees no flaw within himself." The Sages are not suggesting that we are completely unaware of our faults, argues the Rebbe. Indeed, we are very much aware of our flaws and we know our own failings and idiosyncrasies far better than any other person. Yet, this "knowledge" does not naturally develop into self-hatred.

Love has the power to cause a rational person to suspend judgment, and there is no negative reaction caused by man's "knowledge" of his own flaws. Yet, the moment others highlight our faults with this same "knowledge" of our failings, we become enraged. A person does not want to "see," or to be shown, any flaws within himself, and we utterly despise anyone who points out our imperfections and failings.

Says Hillel, this "highlighting" and "pointing out" is precisely what "You shall not do to your fellow." What is hateful to you, namely the substantiation of your failings, don't do unto others.

Love for one's fellow should prevent one's intellectual awareness from creating a negative emotional response. Just as a soul sees no flaws within itself, so too, should it be unable to see flaws within another part of the communal soul. Thus, we can truly love our fellow as our selves.

**INTELLECT VS. EMOTIONS**

Chasidic literature is replete with discussion on the mind's ability to control and inspire the heart and the difficulties inherent in that processes. The addict, for example, may know the hazard and self-damage involved with his habit, yet this knowledge is trapped in the periphery of his consciousness and does not inspire any real change. In Chasidus, this "intellectual ineffectiveness" is treated as a problem in serving G-d and creating a divine state of being. However, when it comes to seeing the faults of our fellow man, employing this very "intellectual ineffectiveness" is the key to good inter-human relations. Thus, knowledge of our fellow's faults, should not produce animosity towards him.

### COSMOLOGICAL ALIGNMENT

The ramifications of the mitzvah to love your fellow as yourself go beyond the realm of good inter-human relations and peaceful societies. The complete unification of the souls of Israel produces the mystical unity of the Holy One, blessed is He, with His *Shechinah*, and the transcendent and immanent manifestations of G-d thereby become one. This unity causes a cosmological alignment in the heavenly spheres; and this, says Hillel, is "the entire Torah."

Ultimately, the Torah was given to facilitate this oneness of G-d with Israel. Then, although G-d sees our conduct, this "Israel-G-d unity" does not permit the divine "knowledge" to arouse the divine attribute of severity or judgment.

However, the Rebbe warns, the disunity of the souls of Israel has the opposite effect, Heaven forbid.

### BE PERFECT WITH THE L-RD

The Rebbe now explains a deeper meaning in the verse "You shall be *tamim* (whole, perfect) with the L-rd your G-d" (Deut. 19:13).

G-d is one with the souls of Israel, and does not "see" any flaws in them. G-d is telling us, that in order to come close to G-d, you shall be whole [and united] with your fellow. Once your soul is enjoined in the communal soul of Israel i.e., you are *tamim*, only then may you approach the divine and unite with G-d during prayer and meditation in the Shema.

### COMMENTARY

In this new light, other mitzvot are seen as specific tools in achieving communion with G-d, while the mitzvah to love your fellow as yourself is fundamental to all divine service. This is why Hillel said "all the rest is but commentary."

The purpose of all mitzvot is to bring about the unity of G-d with His Shechinah, and as explained, the entire foundation for this unity depends upon the love experienced by the souls of Israel toward one another. The mitzvah, "You shall love your fellow as yourself," is thus the basis for the ultimate G-d-Israel unity and all the other mitzvot are a "commentary" expounding and applying this unity.

NOTE ON THE HEBREW TEXT: In vowelizing the Hebrew words in this edition we have followed the grammatical rules of the Holy Tongue, which occasionally differ from the traditional or colloquial pronunciation. The original footnotes to the Hebrew text appear at the end of the maamar.

TRANSLATION
AND
COMMENTARY

Love your fellow like yourself.

—Lev. 19:18[1]

R. Akiva said, "This is a great principle in the Torah."

—*Sifra*, loc cit.[2]

A heathen came to Shammai, wanting to convert to Judaism on the condition that he be taught the entire Torah while standing on one foot. Shammai rejected him with a measuring rod.

He then approached Hillel, who agreed and replied, "What is hateful to you do not do to your fellow. This is the entire Torah—the rest is commentary, go and study."

— *Shabbat* 31a

---

1. *Targum Yonatan ben Uziel:* Love your fellow so that what is hateful to you, you will not inflict upon him. See *Shabbat* 31a; Rambam's *Sefer HaMitzvot*, Positive *Mitzvah* 206 (ed. Heller): "...for him equally (*kamohu*), and all that I abhor for myself, or for my dear ones, I abhor for him just as much (*kamohu*)." Apparently, in some editions, the sentence between the two *kamohu's* was inadvertently omitted.

וְאָהַבְתָּ לְרֵעֲךָ כָּמוֹךָ.

ויקרא יט, יח

רַבִּי עֲקִיבָא אוֹמֵר זֶה כְּלָל גָּדוֹל בַּתּוֹרָה.

ספרא שם

מַעֲשֶׂה בְּנָכְרִי אֶחָד שֶׁבָּא לִפְנֵי שַׁמַּאי אָמַר לוֹ: גַּיְּירֵנִי עַל מְנָת שֶׁתְּלַמְּדֵנִי כָּל הַתּוֹרָה כּוּלָהּ כְּשֶׁאֲנִי עוֹמֵד עַל רֶגֶל אַחַת. דְּחָפוֹ בְּאַמַּת הַבִּנְיָן שֶׁבְּיָדוֹ.
בָּא לִפְנֵי הִלֵּל גַּיְּירֵיהּ. אָמַר לוֹ: דַּעֲלָךְ סָנֵי, לְחַבְרָךְ לָא תַעֲבִיד זוֹ הִיא כָּל הַתּוֹרָה כּוּלָהּ, וְאִידָךְ פֵּירוּשָׁהּ הוּא, זִיל גְּמוֹר.

שבת לא.

---

2. See also *Yerushalmi Nedarim* 9:4; *Bereishit Rabba* end of *parsha* 24, quoted by *Rashi*, in his commentary on *Lev.* 19:18. For the Chabad interpretation see *Or HaTorah, Chukat,* p. 760, and *Pinchas* p. 1120. See also *Kuntres Ahavas Yisrael* (Kehot) for an elaboration on this *mitzvah*.

## THE PROHIBITION AGAINST HATING A FELLOW JEW, AND THE COMMANDMENT TO LOVE A FELLOW JEW

The 238th *mitzvah* [in the enumeration of the 613 *mitzvot* of the Torah][1] is to harbor no enmity toward one's fellow, as it is written: "You shall not hate your brother in your heart."[2] The 243rd *mitzvah* is to love every Jew, as it is written: "Love your fellow man as yourself."[3]

The adage of Hillel the Elder to the would-be proselyte, "What is hateful to you, do not do to your fellow man; this is the entire Torah, the rest is but commentary"[4]—is well-known, but not quite clear. Though we can understand that this *mitzvah* is the essence of precepts between man and his fellow, how can it be said with respect to those between man and G-d? Especially in light of the verse, "If you act righteously, what do you give Him?"[5]

It is also written[6] that it is proper to say before [the morning] prayer, "I hereby accept upon myself to fulfill the positive *mitzvah*, *Love your fellow man as yourself*"—for it is an all-important principle in the service of G-d. [The following exposition will enable us] to understand the meaning of this *mitzvah*.

### I.

ALL ISRAEL ARE ONE

[The student of the Arizal[7] [Rabbi Chaim Vital[8],] writes [in the name of his mentor] in *Sefer Taamei HaMitzvot*, section *Kedoshim*, "All Israel comprises one complete entity within the soul of Adam.

---

1. *Sefer HaChinuch*.
2. Leviticus 19:17.
3. Ibid. 19:18.
4. *Shabbat* 31a.
5. Job 35:7. I.e., how can the efforts of created man influence the Creator?
6. *Siddur Nusach Ha'Ari*, before the beginning of the *Shacharit* Prayer; *Pri Etz Chaim*, "*Shaar Olam HaAsiyah*," ch. 1;

## אִיסּוּר שִׂנְאַת יִשְׂרָאֵל, וּמִצְוַת אַהֲבַת יִשְׂרָאֵל

(קְדוֹשִׁים) שֶׁלֹּא לִשְׂנוֹא לַחֲבֵירוֹ, שֶׁנֶּאֱמַר לֹא תִשְׂנָא אֶת אָחִיךָ בִּלְבָבֶךָ. (וַיִּקְרָא י״ט י״ז) (רל״ח). לֶאֱהוֹב כָּל אָדָם מִיִּשְׂרָאֵל, שֶׁנֶּאֱמַר וְאָהַבְתָּ לְרֵעֲךָ כָּמוֹךָ. (וַיִּקְרָא י״ט י״ח) (רמ״ג):

יָדוּעַ מַאֲמַר הִלֵּל הַזָּקֵן לְהַגֵּר (שַׁבָּת ל״א עַמּוּד א) דַּעֲלָךְ סָנֵי לְחַבְרָךְ לָא תַעֲבִיד זֶהוּ כָּל הַתּוֹרָה כּוּלָהּ וְאִידָךְ פֵּירוּשָׁא הוּא כו' וּבֶאֱמֶת אֵינוּ מוּבָן כָּל כָּךְ דְּהָתֵינַח בְּמִצְוֹת שֶׁבֵּין אָדָם לַחֲבֵירוֹ אֲבָל מִצְוֹת שֶׁבֵּין אָדָם לַמָּקוֹם מַאי אִיכָּא לְמֵימַר וּבִפְרָט שֶׁבּוֹ יִתְבָּרֵךְ כְּתִיב אִם צָדַקְתָּ מַה תִּתֶּן לוֹ (אִיּוֹב ל״ה ז') כַּיָּדוּעַ,

גַּם נוֹדָע מַה שֶׁכָּתוּב שֶׁנָּכוֹן לוֹמַר קוֹדֶם הַתְּפִלָּה הֲרֵינִי מְקַבֵּל עָלַי מִצְוַת עֲשֵׂה שֶׁל וְאָהַבְתָּ לְרֵעֲךָ כָּמוֹךָ לְפִי שֶׁהוּא יְסוֹד גָּדוֹל בַּעֲבוֹדַת ה', וּלְהָבִין עִנְיָנָהּ:

א.

הִנֵּה בְּטַעֲמֵי מִצְוֹת פָּרָשַׁת קְדוֹשִׁים כָּתַב הָאֲרִיזַ״ל וְזֶה לְשׁוֹנוֹ כִּי כָל יִשְׂרָאֵל סוֹד גּוּף אֶחָד שֶׁל נִשְׁמַת אָדָם

---

*Shaar* 3, end of ch. 2; beginning of *Shaar HaKavanot*.

7. ARIZAL (lit., "the lion of blessed memory"): acronym for R. Isaac Luria (1534–1572); universally accepted father of modern kabalistic thought.

8. Primary disciple and exponent of the Arizal's kabbalistic teachings, (1543–1620).

As we have stated elsewhere *(Sefer HaGilgulim* 1:2), each individual Jew constitutes one particular part [of Adam's soul]. This is the basis of the responsibility of one Jew for another if he sins.[9] Accordingly, it was the custom of the Arizal to recite the specific transgressions enumerated in the *Vidui* (Confession)[10] [although he did not, G-d forbid, transgress]; for all Israel is one entity."

Meaning, [the soul of] Adam was the general, all encompassing soul of all the souls of Israel (except those which will descend after the time of the Resurrection, see ibid., ch. 7). He comprised [within his soul] all the souls, some originating in his head, others in his arms,[11] etc.

For this reason he was called Adam—which is [etymologically] related to *edameh l'Elyon*[12], "I will be likened to the One Above."[13] For he was all-encompassing and derived from *Adam de-l'Eila* (Supernal Being)[14] who comprises the Ten *Sefirot* in what is known as *partzuf*[15]. As it is written, "My first-born son Israel,"[16] [and just as a son resembles his father—so Israel (Adam) resembles *Adam de-l'Eila*].

### HEAVENLY UNITY

Elsewhere it is explained [in the exposition[17] of the Zoharic statement, section *Yitro,* "All days receive their blessing..."[18]] that *Adam*

---

9. *Sanhedrin* 27b; *Shavuot* 39b.

10. "We have sinned...we have robbed, etc.," recited after the *Amidah*.

11. Cf. *Tanchuma, Tissa* 12. The soul contains 613 powers and vitalities corresponding to the 613 physical parts of the body. See *Tanya,* Part 1, ch. 51. It is to this spiritual *head* and *arms* that is being referred here.

12. EDAMEH L'ELYON. Earthly man, *adam,* has been created in the image of Supernal Man, *Adam haElyon,* or *Adam de-l'Eila,* referred to in the vision of the Prophet Ezekiel (1:26). Although the etymological origin of the word *adam* is *adamah,* earth, it may also be derived from the verb *damah,* "to be like," from which also the word *demut,* image, is derived. It is fittingly exemplified in the expression, in Isaiah 14:14, *edameh l'eylon,* "I will be like the One Above." See Rabbi Menachem Azaria of Pano, *Asarah Maamarot, Maamar Eim Kol Chai,* part 2, chap. 33; Rabbi Isaiah Horowitz, *Shnei Luchot HaBrit* 3a, 20b, 268b, 301b. See also *Yevamot* 61a.

13. Isaiah 14:14.

14. Based on Ezekiel 1:26.

15. PARTZUF. The ten *sefirot* exist not only

הָרִאשׁוֹן כַּנּוֹדָע אֶצְלֵינוּ (בְּסֵפֶר הַגִּלְגּוּלִים פֶּרֶק א׳ ב׳) וְכָל אֶחָד מִיִּשְׂרָאֵל הוּא אֵבֶר פְּרָטִי וּמִזֶּה הוּא הָעַרְבוּת שֶׁאָדָם עָרֵב בִּשְׁבִיל חֲבֵירוֹ אִם יֶחֱטָא וְלָכֵן נוֹהֵג מוֹרִי זִכְרוֹנוֹ לִבְרָכָה לוֹמַר פְּרָטֵי הַוִּידוּיִים כו׳ כִּי כָל יִשְׂרָאֵל גּוּף אֶחָד עַד כָּאן לְשׁוֹנוֹ

וּבֵיאוּר דְּבָרָיו הוּא שֶׁאָדָם הָרִאשׁוֹן הָיָה כְּלָלוּת כָּל הַנְּשָׁמוֹת כּוּלָם שֶׁבְּיִשְׂרָאֵל (לְבַד מֵאוֹתָן שֶׁיָּבוֹאוּ אַחַר הַתְּחִיָּה עַיֵּן שָׁם פֶּרֶק ז׳) שֶׁהָיָה כּוֹלֵל כּוּלָם מֵהֶם נִתְלִים בְּרֹאשׁוֹ מֵהֶם בִּזְרוֹעוֹ כו׳

וְעַל שֵׁם זֶה נִקְרָא אָדָם אֲדַמֶּה לְעֶלְיוֹן כִּי הוּא בְּחִינָה כְּלָלִית וְנִמְשָׁךְ מִבְּחִינַת אָדָם דִּלְעֵילָּא שֶׁכּוֹלֵל י׳ סְפִירוֹת בִּבְחִינַת פַּרְצוּף וּכְדִכְתִיב בְּנִי בְכוֹרִי יִשְׂרָאֵל (שְׁמוֹת ד׳ כ״ב),

וְהִנֵּה מְבוֹאָר בְּמָקוֹם אַחֵר בְּעִנְיַן אָדָם דִּלְעֵילָּא שֶׁהוּא

---

as individual manifestations of Divine attributes, but are also arranged in various distinct configurations, called *partzufim* ("visages" or "profiles"), each with ten *sefirot* of their own. The *sefirot* are able to interact with each other only as *partzufim*. *Chochmah* (the *partzuf* called *abba*) and *binah* (the *partzuf* called *imma*) are emanated as complete *partzufim* from the start, whereas *z"a* is emanated in its initial form only as comprising the six *sefirot* from *chesed* to *yesod*. It receives its *mochin* (*chochmah* and *binah*) only at a later stage, as an additional light. *Malchut* too, is emanated from the start as a single point only, called *keter malchut*, receiving the other nine *sefirot* only at a later stage.

(This development of *malchut* into a complete *partzuf* is called *binyan hamalchut*, and it is dependent upon the arousal from below (*itaruta d'letatah*) initiated by the Jewish people in this world.) When the radiance of *mochin* (*chochmah* and *binah*) fully illuminates *malchut*, it develops into a state of maturity, becoming an independent, fully functioning, complete *partzuf*. *Malchut* may then be referred to as *nukvah* [female] or *bat* [daughter].

16. Exodus 4:22.

17. *Maamarei Admor Hazaken, Zohar* p. 254.

18. *Zohar* II:88a ff.

*de-l'Eila* corresponds to the Divine Name [whose numerical value is] forty-five מ"ה[19] of [the world of] *Tikkun*.[20] This causes the mutual inclusiveness of each of the Ten *Sefirot*—*chesed* contains *gevurah*, *gevurah* contains *chesed*, and so on.

In [the world of] *Tohu*, however, the *Sefirot* were in a state of separation and disunity. The integration of the *Sefirot* [in *Tikkun*] is effected through the Divine Name מ"ה of *mitzcha*[21] [permeating the

---

19. The four letters of the name *Havaya* may be "spelled" in four different ways. Each spelling yields a different numerical value. The numerical value of *Havaya* when spelled out thus יו"ד ה"א וא"ו ה"א is 45 or מ"ה.

The Divine Name מ"ה causes the integration of the *sefirot*, for this Name connotes *bittul* (self-nullification) as in the verse (Exodus 16:7), "and we are 'what.'" Thus, regarding the *sefirot*, this allows for a state of integrated unity known as the world of *Tikkun*.

20. I.e., the world of *Atzilut*.

TOHU AND TIKKUN: Creation is conceived in Kabbalah and Chasidus in terms of *Giluy Or Ein Sof*, "revelation of the Infinite Light." Together with the metaphor of light, and inseparable from it, is that of *kelim*, "vessels," or "instruments." Light *per se* is invisible; it becomes perceptible only in conjunction with something that reflects the light; i.e. a *keli*, "vessel." Thus, "lights" and "vessels" (*orot v'kelim*) are as inseparable as matter and form. In either case, one is inconceivable without the other. For example, the power of vision is *or*, the eye is the *keli*; the mind is *or*, the brain is *keli*; the idea is *or*, the words conveying it are the *kelim*.

The "light" and the "vessel" must obviously be compatible. The container must fit the contents; no container could contain anything beyond its capacity. If the glare of the light is too strong for the eye, the eye will be "blinded"—it will not see anything and simply will not function. A teacher who wishes to convey an idea (*or*) to a pupil must reduce it to the pupil's mental grasp (*keli*). Otherwise the student would only get confused. Where the capacity of the vessel is overtaxed, the vessel will break, and the contents spilled or scattered.

An analogy: A word consists of two or more letters. When the letters are joined together in the proper order into a word, they form a "vessel" for a concept. If you break up the word into separate letters, the concept vanishes. Now, in the world of *Tohu*, the Divine emanations come forth as separate, distinct and disjointed letters, as it were, each radiating an intense light from its Source in the *Ein Sof*. But in that state the letters cannot form words, or ideas; they are unproductive. The strong, inexorable individuality of the letters has to be reduced, so that they can be put together into word patterns, reflecting their original archetypes though in a reduced intensity.

The Divine attributes—*sefirot*—in their original pristine state, as they emanate from the *Ein Sof*, are absolute, distinct, and mutually exclusive. In this state, *chesed* has no relation to *gevurah*; they are two opposites and incompatible, like fire and water. This early phase of Divine emanation produced the world of

בְּחִינַת שֵׁם מַ"ה דְתִיקוּן שֶׁיִּהְיוּ הַי' סְפִירוֹת כְּלוּלִים זֶה מִזֶּה שֶׁחֶסֶד יִהְיֶה כָּלוּל מִגְּבוּרָה וּגְבוּרָה מֵחֶסֶד וְכַיּוֹצֵא,

מַה שֶּׁאֵין כֵּן בַּתֹּהוּ הָיוּ בִּבְחִינַת פֵּירוּד זֶה תַּחַת זֶה וְהַהִתְכַּלְלוּת הַזֹּאת הוּא עַל יְדֵי הַמְשָׁכַת שֵׁם מַ"ה שֶׁמִּמִּצְחָא שֶׁהוּא בְּחִינַת אֵין סוֹף הַכּוֹלֵל כָּל הַהִשְׁתַּלְשְׁלוּת וּפְרָטֵי

---

*Tohu*. Here the Divine *sefirot* are at the height of their intensity, each one a separate potency, unqualified and unmitigated.

Because the *sefirot* are conceived as two aspects, namely *or* (light) and *keli* (vessel), standing in relation to each other as form to matter, the character of the Divine *sefirot* in *Tohu* is described in terms of "abundance of light and paucity of vessels." In other words, the light was too intense to be controlled or contained. This led to *Shevirat hakelim*, the "breaking of the vessels," a process whereby the intense Divine Light was substantially shut off, as it were, and only "sparks" thereof fell from the upper realm into lower depths.

Thus, the "breaking of the vessels" gave rise to a new, orderly world, called, the World of *Tikkun*, the "repaired" or "restored" world. *Tohu* is described as "abundance of light and a paucity of vessels," and *Tikkun* is described in the reverse, "paucity of light and abundance of vessels."

In *Tikkun* the Divine *sefirot* are integrated and intertwined. The ten *sefirot* can now be classified into two major patterns, *sechel* (intellect) and *middot* (emotions), the former influencing the latter. Under the control of *sechel* the *middot* are ameliorated. No longer can each *middah* be absolute—unlimited *chesed*, or unlimited *gevurah*, but we get *chesed* in *gevurah* and vice versa. The ten Divine *sefirot* now manifest themselves in conglomerate *partzufim* (lit. "faces"), wherein each *sefirah* is composed of ten *sefirot*, and each *sefirah* is in itself a complete entity in terms of the Four Worlds, and all *sefirot* form a complete image, or "face."

21. MITZCHA, or METZACH. Lit., forehead. The *Zohar* (III:262a) mentions three parts, or cavities, of the brain: the front right containing *chochmah*, the front left containing *binah*, and the center (opposite the forehead) containing *Da'at*. The skull that houses and protects the brain corresponds to *keter*, will or desire that transcends intellect. The skull concludes in the *metzach* (forehead) parallel to the part of the brain containing *da'at*, albeit at the front.

*Da'at* is the ability to integrate and harmonize diametrically opposed views or states of being, such as the powers of *chochmah* and *binah*, or the opposing domains of intellect and emotions. The aforementioned culmination of *keter* in *metzach* subsequently permeates the *sefirot*. (*Likkutei Torah*, *Shir Hashirim* 23b)

Thus, while *da'at* is where mental ideas and concepts mature into corresponding dispositions (*middot*) inside the brain, an equivalent outer impression of those ideas can be found outside, on

*Sefirot*]. This is the *Ein Sof*[22] who comprises all the worlds and realms, as well as all the individual beings, as it is written, "All things come from You."[23] Hence, it brings about their coalescence even after they each have emerged into their particular revealed aspects. This is the meaning of what is written in *Tikkunei Zohar*,[24] "The Name מ״ה is the path of *Atzilut*[25]," for just as a path joins two separate places [so the Name מ״ה binds the *Sefirot* one with the other]. See there for a detailed explanation.

## HUMAN UNITY

Similarly, it can be understood how the souls of Israel collectively comprise one complete entity[26], viz., the soul of Adam, which is the general, all-embracing [soul]. Although it contains 248 distinct [spiritual] parts, nevertheless, these parts are mutually inclusive, each containing the others.

By way of analogy, a human body consists of various parts: head, feet, hands, nails, etc., yet each part incorporates all the others. In the hand, there flows, through the interconnecting veins something of the foot's vitality. The same is true of all the other bodily parts. Therefore, as is known, it is possible to cure one part of the body by an injection into another part, because of the confluence of blood in the circulatory system.

This integration of the bodily organs and of the vital forces within them is due to the general life-force that comprises them all. This general life-force dwells[27] in the brain whence it is diffused and

---

the forehead. (*Torah Or*, 83c-d). See *Mystical Concepts in Chassidism*, chapter 3 (Kehot, 1988).

The revelation of G-d's will (*ratzon; keter*) is termed "forehead," and hence the forehead is clear of the concealment of hair, symbolizing revelation. The reasons for G-d's actions, however, remain concealed within the "brain." (*Likkutei Torah, Shelach* 48b)

This revealed state of the Divine Name מ״ה of *mitzcha*, effects and allows the integration of the opposing *sefirot* in the orderly world of *Tikkun*.

In human terms, the forehead reveals man's final "decision" or impression while concealing the intricate details which led to the decision.

22. EIN SOF. Lit. "Infinite," "Endless," meaning the most absolute Infinite force of G-d, totally beyond description, knowledge, and comprehension, completely beyond any boundaries; the Essence of G-d Himself, the innermost aspect of the innermost level of *keter*. *Keter*

הַנִּמְצָאִים כִּי מִמְּךָ הַכֹּל כְּתִיב (דִּבְרֵי הַיָּמִים א' כ"ט י"ד) וְלָכֵן הוּא הַגּוֹרֵם גַּם כֵּן עִנְיַן הַהִתְכַּלְלוּת אַחֲרֵי יְצִיאָתָם אֶל הַגִּלּוּי כָּל אֶחָד וְאֶחָד בִּפְנֵי עַצְמוֹ וְזֶהוּ שֶׁכָּתוּב בְּתִקּוּנֵי זֹהַר שָׁם מ"ה דְּאִיהוּ אֹרַח אֲצִילוּת כְּמוֹ הָאֹרַח שֶׁמְּחַבֵּר שְׁנֵי מְקוֹמוֹת נִבְדָּלִים עַיֵּן שָׁם בַּאֲרוּכָה (בְּבֵאוּר מַאֲמַר הַזֹּהַר פָּרָשַׁת יִתְרוֹ דְּכָל יוֹמִין מִתְבָּרְכִין בֵּיהּ כוּ')

וְעַל דֶּרֶךְ זֶה יוּבַן גַּם כֵּן בְּנִשְׁמוֹת יִשְׂרָאֵל שֶׁהֵם קוֹמָה שְׁלֵמָה בְּיַחַד דְּהַיְנוּ נִשְׁמַת אָדָם הָרִאשׁוֹן שֶׁהִיא כְּלָלוּתָם וְהַגַּם שֶׁיֵּשׁ בָּהּ רַמַ"ח אֵיבָרִים מְיֻחָדִים הֲרֵי הֵם כְּלוּלִים זֶה מִזֶּה

וּכְמוֹ עַל דֶּרֶךְ מָשָׁל בְּגוּף אֶחָד שֶׁהֲגַם שֶׁהוּא בְּהִתְחַלְּקוּת צִיּוּר אֵיבָרִים רֹאשׁ וְרַגְלַיִם וְיָדַיִם וְצִפָּרְנַיִם מִכָּל מָקוֹם כָּל אֶחָד כָּלוּל מִזּוּלָתוֹ שֶׁבַּיָּד יֵשׁ חַיּוּת מֵעֵין הָרֶגֶל עַל יְדֵי הַוְּרִידִים שֶׁנִּמְשְׁכוּ בּוֹ וְכֵן בִּשְׁאָר כָּל הָאֵיבָרִים וּכַנּוֹדָע שֶׁמְּרַפְּאִים אֵבֶר אֶחָד עַל יְדֵי הַקָּזָה בַּחֲבֵרוֹ מִצַּד עֵרוּב הַדָּמִים

וְהַהִתְכַּלְלוּת הַזֹּאת בְּאֵיבְרֵי הַגּוּף וּבְחַיּוּת הַנֶּפֶשׁ שֶׁבָּהֶם הוּא מֵחֲמַת כְּלָלוּת הַחַיּוּת שֶׁכּוֹלֵל כּוּלָּם שֶׁהוּא הַמֵּאִיר בַּמּוֹחַ

---

(Will) is the intermediary between the *Ein Sof* and the *Sefirot*.

23. I Chronicles, 29:14.

24. Introduction. *Tikkunei Zohar* consists of seventy chapters on the first word of the Torah, by the school of Rabbi Shimon bar Yochai (circa. 120 c.e.). First printed in Mantua, 1558, *Tikkunei Zohar* contains some of the most important discussions in *Kabbalah*, and is essential for understanding the *Zohar*.

25. *Atzilut*, world of "Emanation," highest of the Four Worlds, in Chabad etymologically connected with *etzel* ("near"), i.e. nearest to the Source of creation, the *Ein Sof*, hence still in a state of infinity. See *Mystical Concepts in Chassidism*, chapter 4 (*Kehot*, 1988).

26. See *Likkutei Torah*, beg *Nitzavim* (44a).

27. Literally, irradiates.

individualized,[28] but contains them all. (As for example, the unformed hylic matter, "hyle")

For this reason the brain perceives the pain of all the 248 organs, and [to the brain] the pain of the arm and of the leg are similar. Indeed, at times the brain senses more acutely the pain of a wound to the nail than the pain of a wound to the hand, as can be observed.

## ADAM'S SOUL

Similarly, the coalescence of the 248 parts of Adam's soul, one with the other, is due to the source of his soul's vitality deriving from the Supernal Wisdom of the Supernal Being, the blessed *Ein Sof*. G-d abides in, and is united with, His Wisdom, for "He and His Wisdom are all one."[29]

Therefore, it is written, "My first-born son." Just as a son is derived from a drop deriving from his father's brain [so, too, his soul is derived from His Wisdom].[30] However, after Adam's soul was divided into numerous root-souls, which in turn were subdivided into manifold branches and *sparks* in individual bodies, the soul's state is analogous to bodily organs which have become severed one from the other. In this state, the pain of the foot is no longer felt by the hand.

## CORPOREAL DIVISION

But the separation [between one Jew and another] exists only in respect to the body. As parts of a comprehensive whole, their souls are never truly separated, analogous to a hand that has veins linking it to the legs and eyes, and the foot to the hand. Accordingly, the hand, for example, feels an intense pain, in a spiritual sense, from the pain of the eye, as mentioned above.

Hence, the Arizal would recite confession (*viduy*) for all the transgressions that any Jew may have committed. For the part [in the General Soul] in which that Jew's soul was rooted, was suffering, and this pain was transmitted to the higher parts where the soul of the Arizal was rooted. How much more so is this true with respect to the Source of our souls, i.e., "the brain of the Father and His blessed

---

28. See *Tanya*, Part 1, ch. 51.   29. *Hilchot Yesodei HaTorah* 2:10. *Cf.*

שֶׁבָּרֹאשׁ שֶׁמִּמֶּנּוּ נִתְפָּרְדוּ כָּל אֶחָד לְעַצְמוֹ וְהוּא כּוֹלֵל כּוּלָּם דֶּרֶךְ מָשָׁל הַהִיּוּלִי כַּיָּדוּעַ

וְלָכֵן הַמּוֹחַ הוּא הַמַּרְגִּישׁ כָּל כְּאֵבֵי הָרַמַ"ח אֵיבָרִים וּכְאֵב הַיָּד עִם הָרֶגֶל שָׁוִים אֶצְלוֹ אַדְּרַבָּה לִפְעָמִים יַרְגִּישׁ הַמּוֹחַ יוֹתֵר כְּאֵב מַכָּה שֶׁבַּצִּפּוֹרֶן מִכְּאֵב מַכָּה שֶׁבַּיָּד כַּנִּרְאֶה בַּחוּשׁ,

וְעַל דֶּרֶךְ זֶה הָיָה הַהִתְכַּלְלוּת בְּרַמַ"ח אֵיבְרֵי נֶפֶשׁ אָדָם הָרִאשׁוֹן זֶה מִזֶּה מֵחֲמַת מְקוֹר חַיֵּי נַפְשׁוֹ שֶׁהוּא מִבְּחִינַת חָכְמָה עִילָּאָה דְּאָדָם הָעֶלְיוֹן בִּבְחִינַת אֵין סוֹף בָּרוּךְ הוּא שֶׁשּׁוֹרֶה וּמִתְיַחֵד בְּחָכְמָתוֹ שֶׁהוּא וְחָכְמָתוֹ אֶחָד

וְלָכֵן נֶאֱמַר בְּנִי בְּכוֹרִי וּכְמוֹ הַבֵּן שֶׁהוּא טִפָּה מִמּוֹחַ הָאָב, אַךְ אָמְנָם לְאַחַר שֶׁנִּתְחַלְּקָה נִשְׁמַת אָדָם הָרִאשׁוֹן לְשָׁרָשִׁים רַבִּים וְכָל אֶחָד נֶחֱלַק לַעֲנָפִים וּלְנִיצוֹצוֹת רַבּוֹת בְּגוּפוֹת מְיוּחָדוֹת הֲרֵי זֶה כְּמָשָׁל הָאֵיבָרִים שֶׁנִּפְרְדוּ זֶה מִזֶּה וְלֹא יִכְאַב לְהַיָּד מַכָּה שֶׁבָּרֶגֶל הַמּוּפְרֶדֶת מִמֶּנּוּ וְכַיּוֹצֵא,

אָמְנָם הַפֵּירוּד הַזֶּה הוּא רַק מִצַּד הַגּוּף אֲבָל הַנֶּפֶשׁ לֹא נִפְרְדָה בֶּאֱמֶת וְכוּלָּם מַתְאִימוֹת וּכְמָשָׁל הַיָּד שֶׁיֵּשׁ בָּהּ מוֹרִידֵי הָרֶגֶל וְהָעַיִן וְכֵן בָּרֶגֶל מִן הַיָּד כוּ' וְכַיּוֹצֵא וְיֵשׁ לָהּ כְּאֵב עָצוּם בְּרוּחָנִיּוּתָהּ מִכְּאֵב הָעַיִן כַּנַּ"ל בְּמָשָׁל

וְלָכֵן אָמַר הָאֲרִיזַ"ל כָּל פְּרָטֵי הַוִּידּוּיִם שֶׁחָטָא אֶחָד מִיִּשְׂרָאֵל שֶׁהֲרֵי הוּא כְּאֵב אוֹתוֹ אֵבָר שֶׁבּוֹ מוּשְׁרֶשֶׁת נֶפֶשׁ אוֹתוֹ הַיִּשְׂרָאֵל וּמַגִּיעַ הַכְּאֵב גַּם לְאֵבָר הָעֶלְיוֹן שֶׁמּוּשְׁרָשׁ נֶפֶשׁ הָאֲרִיזַ"ל וּבִפְרָט מִצַּד מְקוֹר נִשְׁמוֹתֵינוּ מוֹחַ הָאָב

---

*Tanya*, Part 1, ch. 2.    30. Cf. *Tanya, loc cit.*

Wisdom"[31] which comprises all the 248 parts, and perceives their discomfort.

## COMMANDMENT AND EFFECT

We are therefore commanded to love every individual Jew, since each one includes all the souls of Israel, as in the above analogy of the bodily organs. Thus, a person incorporates also his fellow, so he should love his fellow as he does himself. Similarly, he is incorporated within his fellow, as mentioned above with reference to the inter-connection of the body's organs.[32]

For this reason also one must accept upon himself this *mitzvah* before beginning to pray. One is thereby able to offer one's soul to G-d in [the recital of the word] *Echad* [*one*—in *Keriat Shema*] so that it rise before Him in the manner of *mayin nukvin*[33] in *Keriat Shema*. This elevation can be achieved only when the soul is complete and "healthy." Namely, when it unites with all the souls—just as a bodily organ is healthy when its veins that link it to all the organs are healthy. Then [his soul] can ascend in favor before G-d in His blessed Wisdom, which contains all the souls actually as one. Inasmuch as his soul is also unified with all others, it can ascend into the general, all encompassing Light that is its source and root.

This unity is achieved when a man demonstrates his unreserved love for his fellow—as the interconnection of the bodily organs one with the other—[with a feeling of] "what is mine is yours"[34] for he is his "bone and flesh."[35] If, however, he feels enmity in his heart for a fellow Jew, he sunders from his soul that part of his fellow contained within him, rejecting him by this hatred and removing his will from him.

He thereby blemishes and mars his own soul, for now this part is lacking in him. He thus becomes defective—since every individual part is comprised of all the 613, and through his hatred, he

---

31. Cf. *Tanya, loc cit.*

32. See *Jerusalem Talmud, Nedarim*, 9:4.

33. MAYIN NUKVIN: Lit., Feminine waters. "Male" and "female" are terms used in Kabbalah to denote "giver" and "recipient," respectively. "Feminine waters" therefore denotes benevolent acts, self inspired, rising from man to G-d, while "masculine waters" denotes the flow of influence and grace from G-d to man. See also *Zohar* I:29b.

וְחָכְמָתוֹ יִתְבָּרֵךְ הַכּוֹלֵל אֶת כּוּלָם וּמַרְגִּישׁ כְּאֵב כָּל הָרַמַ"ח אֵיבָרִים,

וְלָכֵן נִצְטַוֵּינוּ גַם כֵּן לֶאֱהוֹב כָּל אָדָם מִיִּשְׂרָאֵל שֶׁהֲרֵי כָּל אָדָם כָּלוּל מִכָּל נִשְׁמוֹת יִשְׂרָאֵל כַּנַ"ל מִן הָאֵיבָרִים וַהֲרֵי אִם כֵּן בּוֹ יֵשׁ זוּלָתוֹ גַם כֵּן וְיֶאֱהַב זוּלָתוֹ כָּמוֹהוּ וְכֵן הוּא כָּלוּל בְּזוּלָתוֹ כַּנַ"ל בְּקִישׁוּר הָאֵיבָרִים,

וְזֶהוּ גַם כֵּן שֶׁצָּרִיךְ לְקַבֵּל עָלָיו מִצְוָה זוֹ קוֹדֶם הַתְּפִלָּה כְּדֵי שֶׁיּוּכַל לִמְסוֹר נַפְשׁוֹ בְּאֶחָד שֶׁתַּעֲלֶה לִפְנֵי ה' בִּבְחִינַת מַ"ן [מַיִין נוּקְבִין] בִּקְרִיאַת שְׁמַע וְאִי אֶפְשָׁר לִהְיוֹת עֲלִיָּה זוֹ אֶלָּא אִם כֵּן תִּהְיֶה שְׁלֵימָה וּבְרִיאָה' דְּהַיְינוּ שֶׁתִּהְיֶה כְּלוּלָה מִכָּל הַנְּשָׁמוֹת שֶׁהוּא כְּמוֹ הָאֵיבָר שֶׁבְּרִיאוּתוֹ הוּא כְּשֶׁבְּרִיאִים הַוְוֵרִידִים שֶׁבּוֹ הַכְּלוּלִים מִכָּל הָאֵיבָרִים, שֶׁאָז תַּעֲלֶה לָרָצוֹן לִפְנֵי ה' בְּחָכְמָתוֹ יִתְבָּרֵךְ שֶׁהִיא הַכּוֹלֶלֶת כָּל הַנְּשָׁמוֹת כּוּלָן כְּאֶחָד מַמָּשׁ, שֶׁלְּפִי שֶׁהַנְּשָׁמָה יֵשׁ בָּהּ בְּהִתְכַּלְלוּת גַם כֵּן מִכּוּלָם יְכוֹלָה הִיא לַעֲלוֹת בָּאוֹר הַכְּלָלִי שֶׁהוּא מְקוֹרָן וְשָׁרְשָׁן,

וְהַהִתְכַּלְלוּת זֹאת הוּא כְּשֶׁהָאָדָם מַרְאֶה בְּעַצְמוֹ וּבְגוּפוֹ כֵּן שֶׁאוֹהֵב רֵעֵהוּ כְּאֵיבָרִים הַכְּלוּלִים זֶה מִזֶּה וְשֶׁלִּי שֶׁלָּךְ כִּי עַצְמוֹ וּבְשָׂרוֹ הוּא, מַה שֶׁאֵין כֵּן כְּשֶׁשּׂוֹנֵא לְאֶחָד מִיִּשְׂרָאֵל בְּלִבּוֹ הֲרֵי הוּא מַפְרִיד מִנַּפְשׁוֹ אוֹתוֹ חֵלֶק שֶׁל זוּלָתוֹ הַכָּלוּל בּוֹ וְדוֹחֲהוּ מֵעָלָיו בְּשִׂנְאָה זוֹ שֶׁשְּׂנֵאוֹ וּמְסַלֵּק רְצוֹנוֹ מִמֶּנּוּ

וּמִמֵּילָא יֵשׁ פְּגָם וְחִסָּרוֹן בְּנַפְשׁוֹ שֶׁנֶּחְסַר בּוֹ הַחֵלֶק הַנַ"ל וְנַעֲשֶׂה בַּעַל מוּם כִּי בֶּאֱמֶת כָּל אֵיבָר פְּרָטִי כָּלוּל מִתַּרְיַ"ג

---

The essentially Lurianic concept of the elevation of the feminine waters (מ"ן) is the "arousal from below," which consequently elicits the masculine waters (מ"ד, *mayin dechurin*)—the "arousal from above," to issue and effuse downwards "to feed and be received by the category of the feminine." See *Eitz Chaim* 39:1; *Tanya*, end of chapters 10 and 53.

34. *Avot* 5:10.

35. Cf. Genesis 29:14.

severs from himself that individual part. He is then unable to ascend in favor before G-d; as it is written: "He who has a blemish shall not approach to offer..."[36] For the *Or Ein Sof,* blessed is He, Who comprises them all, will not tolerate him because of the flaw within him, being deficient of that individual—for the *Or Ein Sof* comprises that missing individual as well. This should suffice for the intelligent.

That is why we have been commanded with several prohibitions against the offering by blemished *Kohanim* and against defective sacrifices themselves, as they are described in the portion *Emor.*[37] We have likewise been enjoined with a positive precept to offer every sacrifice unblemished, as it is written, "To be accepted, it shall be perfect; it shall have no blemish."[38]

## II.

HILLEL AND ONKELOS

We have, thus, clearly elucidated the reason for this *mitzvah* [of *ahavat Yisrael*]. Yet, based upon an exposition of the above-mentioned statement of Hillel, there is another wonderful explanation. It, too, elucidates the profound goodness that one accomplishes for himself and for the entire world through observing this positive *mitzvah.* It also explains the opposite, G-d forbid, when one neglects it and transgresses the negative injunction of the Torah, "You shall not hate."

Let us understand why Hillel paraphrased this *mitzvah* in the negative: *What is hateful to you do not do to your fellow,* and did not state it in the positive, as did Onkelos[39] in his rendition: *Love your fellow as yourself.* The answer is that in this way Hillel interpreted this *mitzvah* in a deeper sense, as follows.

SELF-LOVE

[The Talmudic statement that] "A person sees no flaw within

---

36. Leviticus 21:17.

37. Ibid. 22:17 ff.

38. Ibid. 22:21.

39. Onkelos (2nd century c.e.), a proselyte of Roman origin, authored *Targum Onkelos,* an Aramaic translation of the Torah, under the guidance of Rabbi Eliezer

וְהַיְנוּ מֵהִתְכַּלְלוּת זוּלָתוֹ בּוֹ וְעַל יְדֵי הַשִּׂנְאָה הוּא מַפְרִיד מִמֶּנּוּ אוֹתוֹ חֵלֶק הַפְּרָטִי וְאָז אֵינוֹ יָכוֹל לַעֲלוֹת לְרָצוֹן לִפְנֵי ה' וּכְדִכְתִיב אֲשֶׁר יִהְיֶה בּוֹ מוּם לֹא יַקְרִיב לְהַקְרִיב כו' (וַיִּקְרָא כ"א י"ז) שֶׁאוֹר אֵין סוֹף בָּרוּךְ הוּא הַכּוֹלֵל כּוּלָם לֹא יְסַבְּלֶנּוּ מִצַּד הַחִסָּרוֹן שֶׁבּוֹ שֶׁחִסֵּר אוֹתוֹ [הָאֵבֶר] הַפְּרָטִי שֶׁהֲרֵי אֵין סוֹף בָּרוּךְ הוּא כּוֹלֵל גַּם אוֹתוֹ וְדַי לְמֵבִין.

וְלָכֵן נִצְטַוֵּינוּ כַּמָּה לֹא תַעֲשֶׂה בְּהַקְרָבַת בַּעֲלֵי מוּמִים הֵן בַּכֹּהֲנִים הֵן בַּקָּרְבָּנוֹת עַצְמָן כְּמוֹ שֶׁכָּתוּב בְּפָרָשַׁת אֱמוֹר וְנִצְטַוֵּינוּ גַּם כֵּן בְּמִצְוַת עֲשֵׂה לְהַקְרִיב כָּל קָרְבָּן תָּמִים כְּדִכְתִיב תָּמִים יִהְיֶה לְרָצוֹן כו' (וַיִּקְרָא כ"ב כ"א):

ב.

וְאַף עַל פִּי שֶׁנִּתְבָּאֵר הֵיטֵב טוּב טַעַם לְמִצְוָה זוֹ עֲדַיִן יֵשׁ בָּזֶה עוֹד טַעַם נִפְלָא בְּעוֹצֶם הַטּוֹבָה שֶׁהָאָדָם עוֹשֶׂה לוֹ וּלְכָל הָעוֹלָם בְּקִיּוּם מִצְוַת עֲשֵׂה זוֹ וּלְהִיפּוּךְ חַס וְשָׁלוֹם כְּשֶׁמְּבַטֵּל מִצְוַת עֲשֵׂה זוֹ וְעוֹבֵר עַל לֹא תַעֲשֶׂה שֶׁל תּוֹרָה דְּלֹא תִשְׂנָא:

וְהַיְנוּ עַל פִּי בֵּיאוּר מַאֲמַר הִלֵּל הַנִּזְכָּר לְעֵיל שֶׁאֵינוֹ מוּבָן גַּם כֵּן לָמָּה כֵּן בֵּיאֲרוּ מִצְוַת עֲשֵׂה זוֹ בְּעִנְיַן הַשְּׁלִילָה מַה דְּסָנֵי עֲלָךְ לְחַבְרָךְ לָא תַעֲבִיד וְלֹא אָמַר לוֹ הַהֵן שֶׁבָּהּ הַנִּגְלֶה מִפְּשַׁט הַכָּתוּב כִּדְתַרְגֵּם אוּנְקְלוֹס וְתִרְחֲמֵיהּ לְחַבְרָךְ כְּוָתָךְ. וְהָעִנְיָן כִּי דְּבָרָיו אֵלֶּה הוּא פֵּירוּשׁ מִצְוַת וְאָהַבְתָּ לְרֵעֲךָ כָּמוֹךָ בְּעִנְיָן עָמוֹק,

דְּהַיְנוּ כְּמוֹ שֶׁאֵין אָדָם רוֹאֶה לְעַצְמוֹ חוֹב אֵין הַפֵּירוּשׁ שֶׁאֵינוֹ יוֹדֵעַ כְּלָל חוֹבוֹתָיו אַדְּרַבָּה יוּכַל לִרְאוֹת וּלְהָבִין הֵיטֵב

himself"[40] does not mean that a person is completely unaware of his shortcomings. On the contrary, he may be aware of and comprehend the depths of his deficiency even more than another person. For someone else perceives only what is visible to the eye, while he discerns what is in the depths of his own heart.

The meaning, then, is that his fault is of no importance to him, and therefore does not disturb him. It is as if he does not see it at all, for his great self-love covers all his shortcomings.[41] Though intellectually aware of his deficiencies, he relegates them to a superficial, peripheral status, not allowing them to evoke a corresponding emotional feeling [of distress]. Accordingly, his shortcomings give him no cause to be concerned. Any fault becomes submerged in, and nullified by, his intense self-love and is dismissed to a state of latency.

Now, should another person perceive his fault, he is enraged, although he himself is well aware of it. Essentially, his anger is not aroused by the fact that the other person is mistaken in his judgment [suspecting him of a nonexistent defect]—for, indeed, he is aware of his shortcoming. Rather, the other person's perceiving of his defect renders it concrete and substantial, whereas when he alone knows of it, his self-love conceals it. He is angered that his friend revealed his flaw from its previously concealed and unfelt state (due to his self-love). But now, as far as his friend is concerned, it has become a definite and substantive shortcoming.

HILLEL'S ELUCIDATION

This, then [is what Hillel says], "what is hateful to you," namely, the revelation [of a shortcoming]—"do not do to your fellow"—do not perceive his faults and imperfections, whether in his social conduct or in his spiritual behavior, to consider them concrete and substantial. Instead, let your love for him be so great that it covers his flaw; do not permit the flaw to move from intellectual awareness to a negative emotional feeling.

When a person feels exceedingly great affection and goodwill for

---

40. *Shabbat* 119a.   41. Cf. Proverbs 10:12.

עַמְקוּת פְּחִיתוּתוֹ יוֹתֵר מֵרָאיִת זוּלָתוֹ עָלָיו שֶׁהֲרֵי זוּלָתוֹ אֵינוֹ רוֹאֶה אֶלָּא לָעֵינַיִם וְהוּא יִרְאֶה לַלֵּבָב.

אֶלָּא הַכַּוָּנָה שֶׁאֵין הַחוֹב תּוֹפֵס מָקוֹם אֶצְלוֹ כְּלָל לְהִתְפָּעֵל מִזֶּה וּכְאִלּוּ אֵינוֹ רוֹאֶה אוֹתוֹ כְּלָל כִּי מִפְּנֵי הָאַהֲבָה הַגְּדוֹלָה אֲשֶׁר הוּא אוֹהֵב מְאֹד אֶת עַצְמוֹ עַל כָּל פְּשָׁעָיו שֶׁיּוֹדֵעַ בְּדַעְתּוֹ תְּכַסֶּה הָאַהֲבָה בִּבְחִינַת מַקִּיף שֶׁלֹּא יוּמְשַׁךְ מִן הַיְדִיעָה לִידֵי הִתְפָּעֲלוּת בַּמִּדּוֹת וְלָכֵן אֵין תּוֹפְסִים מָקוֹם כְּלָל לְהִתְפָּעֵל מִזֶּה, וְזֶהוּ שֶׁאֵינוֹ רוֹאֶה חוֹב לְעַצְמוֹ שֶׁנִּשְׁקָע וְנִתְבַּטֵּל בְּהָאַהֲבָה רַבָּה הַמְכַסָּה עַל כָּל הַפְּשָׁעִים בִּבְחִינַת מַקִּיף,

וְכַאֲשֶׁר יִרְאֶה זוּלָתוֹ עַל הַחוֹב שֶׁלּוֹ וְיָבִין אוֹתוֹ יִרְגַּז מְאֹד אַף עַל פִּי שֶׁיּוֹדֵעַ בְּעַצְמוֹ שֶׁאֱמֶת הוּא וְהַיְנוּ לְפִי שֶׁעִקַּר רוּגְזוֹ אֵינוֹ עַל עֶצֶם הַפְּחִיתוּת שֶׁחֲבֵירוֹ מְדַמֶּה שֶׁקֶּר שֶׁהֲרֵי יוֹדֵעַ שֶׁאֱמֶת הוּא רַק עַל שֶׁיְּדִיעַת חֲבֵירוֹ אֶת פְּחִיתוּתוֹ הוּא בִּבְחִינַת יֵשׁ וְהִתְפָּעֲלוּת, מַה שֶּׁאֵין כֵּן כְּשֶׁהוּא יוֹדֵעַ הָאַהֲבָה מְכַסָּה, וְיִרְגַּז עַל חֲבֵירוֹ עַל הַהִתְגַּלּוּת שֶׁגִּילָּה חֲבֵירוֹ הַחוֹב שֶׁלּוֹ מִתּוֹךְ הַסֵּתֶר וְכִסּוּי הָאַהֲבָה שֶׁהָיְתָה מְכַסָּה עָלָיו וְלֹא הָיָה נִרְאֶה כְּלָל וְעַתָּה אֵצֶל חֲבֵירוֹ נִרְאֶה לְיֵשׁ וּדְבַר מָה,

וְזֶהוּ מַה דְּסָנֵי לָךְ גִּילּוּי זֶה, לְחַבְרָךְ לֹא תַעֲבִיד שֶׁלֹּא תַרְאֶה חוֹבוֹתָיו וּפְשָׁעָיו, הֵן בְּמִילֵּי דְעָלְמָא בִּדְבָרִים שֶׁבֵּין אָדָם לַחֲבֵירוֹ וְהֵן בְּמִילֵּי דִשְׁמַיָּא, לְיֵשׁ וּדְבַר מָה אֶלָּא מָה יִהְיֶה הָאַהֲבָה שֶׁלְּךָ לוֹ גְּדוֹלָה כָּל כָּךְ עַד שֶׁתְּכַסֶּה עַל הַפְּשָׁעִים וְלֹא תַנִּיחַ אוֹתָם מִן הַיְדִיעָה לָבֹא לְהִתְפָּעֲלוּת בַּמִּדּוֹת

וּכְמוֹ כַּאֲשֶׁר יִהְיֶה לָאָדָם רָצוֹן וּתְשׁוּקָה נִפְלָאָה לַחֲבֵירוֹ מִצַּד הַמְשָׁכָה רַבָּה וַעֲצוּמָה שֶׁמֵּעַצְמִיּוּת הַנֶּפֶשׁ שֶׁיֵּשׁ לוֹ אֵלָיו כָּל אֲשֶׁר יַעֲשֶׂה לוֹ רָעוֹת הִיפּוּךְ אַהֲבָתוֹ לֹא יִהְיוּ תּוֹפְסִים

another, [a love] issuing from the very essence of his soul, any wrong the other may inflict upon him will have no significance. It will be nullified in the great intensity of his love—"surging waters cannot extinguish the love..."[42]

Therefore, Hillel declared, "This is the whole Torah." For the complete unity of the souls of Israel, as if a single entity, evokes a most wondrous effect Above, which is the essence and purpose of the entire Torah. That is, the unity of the Holy One, blessed is He, with His *Shechinah*[43]. His *Shechinah* is synonymous with *imma tata'ah*[44] and *matronita*,[45] the source of Jewish souls. "The beauty of Jacob was similar to Adam's," [state our Sages].[46] This means that Jacob, who incorporated all the souls, is akin to the beauty of *Adam haElyon* (the Supernal Being) upon His Throne, "the appearance of the likeness of G-d's Glory,"[47] for "His people is a part of the L-rd."[48]

CAUSE AND EFFECT

When the souls of Israel join and unite, this in turn unites the *One* [G-d] with *one* [Israel]. That is, G-d becomes united with Israel. Once this union occurs, the Supernal Being sees no deficiency within Himself, and He removes every transgression of Israel, as "one who cleanses in the mighty ocean."[49] And as it is written, "He beholds no sin in Jacob and sees no wrongdoing in Israel"[50] for "the L-rd his G-d is with him;" and Man does not see, metaphorically speaking, his own fault. This should suffice for the intelligent.

---

42. Song of Songs 8:7.

43. SHECHINAH, Divine Presence, is the immanent manifestation of the Divine influence, that dwells on earth through the righteous who study the Torah and perform *mitzvot*. In addition to *Shechinah* being identified with *malchut* and the source of the souls, *Shechinah* corresponds to the second letter *hay* of the Tetragrammaton, Y-H-V-H. The sinner, on the other hand, disrupts the unity of the Divine Name, dragging the *Shechinah* into "exile."

44. IMMA TATA'AH. Lit. lower matriarch. Kabbalistic literature abounds with allegorical human terms, and references to categories represented by symbolic terms as "masculine" (generally: the emanating influencing aspect), and feminine (generally: the recipient aspect); see *Zohar* I:157b; cf. *Bava Batra* 74b; *Shomer Emunim* I:26f. These terms apply generally to the *sefirot*: *chochmah* is *abba* (father); *binah* is *imma* (mother; or *imma ila'ah*, superior mother), the lower *sefirot* are the "children": *da'at*, *tiferet*, or the *midot*

מָקוֹם כְּלָל וּבְטֵלִים נֶגֶד הָאַהֲבָה רַבָּה מַיִם רַבִּים לֹא יוּכְלוּ כוּ׳ (שִׁיר הַשִּׁירִים ח׳ ז׳),

וְלָכֵן זֶהוּ כָּל הַתּוֹרָה כּוּלָהּ שֶׁעַל יְדֵי הִתְכַּלְלוּת נִשְׁמוֹת יִשְׂרָאֵל אֵלוּ בְּאֵלוּ וְהָיוּ לַאֲחָדִים מַמָּשׁ כְּאִילוּ הִיא קוֹמָה אַחַת לְבַד עַל יְדֵי זֶה גּוֹרֵם לְמַעְלָה עִנְיָן נִפְלָא שֶׁהוּא יְסוֹד וְתַכְלִית כָּל הַתּוֹרָה כּוּלָהּ וְהוּא עִנְיַן יְחוּד קוּדְשָׁא בְּרִיךְ הוּא וּשְׁכִינְתֵּיהּ שֶׁשְּׁכִינְתֵּיהּ הִיא אִימָא תַּתָּאָה וּמַטְרוֹנִיתָא מְקוֹר נִשְׁמוֹת יִשְׂרָאֵל, כִּי הִנֵּה שׁוּפְרֵיהּ דְּיַעֲקֹב מֵעֵין שׁוּפְרֵיהּ דְּאָדָם (בָּבָא מְצִיעָא פ״ד א׳) וּפֵירוּשׁ שֶׁיַּעֲקֹב הָיָה כְּלָלוּת כָּל הַנְּשָׁמוֹת הוּא מֵעֵין שׁוּפְרֵיהּ דְּאָדָם הָעֶלְיוֹן שֶׁעַל הַכִּסֵּא הוּא מַרְאֵה דְּמוּת כְּבוֹד ה׳ (יְחֶזְקֵאל א׳ כ״ח) כִּי חֵלֶק ה׳ עַמּוֹ (דְּבָרִים ל״ב ט׳)

וּכְשֶׁמִּתְכַּלְלִים נִשְׁמוֹת יִשְׂרָאֵל וְהָיוּ לַאֲחָדִים עַל יְדֵי זֶה נַעֲשֶׂה אֶחָד בְּאֶחָד שֶׁה׳ יִתְבָּרֵךְ מִתְיַחֵד עִם הַיִּשְׂרָאֵל וְהָיוּ לַאֲחָדִים וְאֵין הָאָדָם דִּלְעֵילָא רוֹאֶה חוֹב לְעַצְמוֹ וְאָז הוּא עוֹבֵר עַל כָּל פֶּשַׁע שֶׁל הַיִּשְׂרָאֵל כְּמַאן דְּמִסְתְּחֵי בְּיַמָּא רַבָּא וּכְמוֹ שֶׁכָּתוּב לֹא הִבִּיט אָוֶן בְּיַעֲקֹב וְלֹא רָאָה עָמָל בְּיִשְׂרָאֵל (בַּמִּדְבָּר כ״ג כ״א) מִפְּנֵי שֶׁה׳ אֱלֹקָיו עִמּוֹ וְאֵין הָאָדָם רוֹאֶה עַל דֶּרֶךְ מָשָׁל חוֹבַת עַצְמוֹ וְדַי לַמֵּבִין

---

from *chesed* to *yesod* as a whole correspond to *ben* (son); and *malchut* to *bat* (daughter; or *imma tata'ah*, the lower mother); see *Zohar* III:290a ff; *Pardes Rimonim* 8:17. See further *Tanya*, Bi-Lingual Edition, *Iggeret Hakodesh*, sect. 20, note 62.

45. *Matronita*, translated as "queen," corresponds to *malchut*, source of the souls of Israel, as it states (*Mishna, Shabbat* 14:4) "all of Israel are princes." (*B'Shaah Shehikdimu 5672*, vol. 2, p. 892)

46. *Bava Metzia* 84a, where is states "the Patriarch Jacob." However, *Iggeret Hakodesh* 7 (*Tanya* p. 222) quotes this aphorism as stated here. See footnotes 22-23 there.

47. Ezekiel 1:26, 28. See footnote 12.

48. Deuteronomy 32:9.

49. Cf. *Zohar*, III, p. 132b.

50. Numbers 23:21.

The meaning of the phrase, "He beholds no...and sees no..." is not that they are concealed from Him, G-d forbid. For everything is revealed and known to Him, even one's trivial conversations.[51] Rather it means, as it is written, "He sees iniquity but takes no notice of it."[52] The attribute of severity and judgment is not aroused by His infinite and boundless knowledge [of their wrong doings]. For His love covers it, as it is written, "And G-d (אלוה) screened for him."[53] אלוה (G-d) is a composite of אל־ו״ה which refers to the supernal kindness which encompasses, (and which is a garment of the soul and its seal), as is explained in *Eitz Chaim*[54].

This is not the case, however, when, G-d forbid, the Jewish people are disunited. "Anyone who has within him a defect shall not approach to offer" and he causes, thereby, disunity Above (between the Holy One, blessed is He, and the *Shechinah*, the Community of Israel). Then He will see the flaw, and that person's flaw in particular, for it was he who caused this disunity, Heaven forbid.

[The Divine blessings are contingent upon the unity of Israel, as we say in the *Amidah*,] "Bless us, our Father, all of us as *one*"; with the result that, "You are wholly beautiful, My beloved, and there is no blemish in you."[55] This brings about the unity of the Holy One, blessed is He, with His *Shechinah*, i.e., the revelation of *Or Ein Sof* within the source of the souls of Israel to be "One with one."

G-D AND ISRAEL UNITE

This is the deeper meaning of the verse, "You shall be *tamim* (whole, perfect) with the L-rd your G-d."[56] G-d is in a state of completeness [and unity] with the totality of the souls of Israel. In other words, the radiance of the Supernal Wisdom [shines] into the totality of the parts of the *Shechinah*—[fulfilling] "You shall love your fellow as yourself," and does not behold his flaws. So, too, you shall be whole [and united] with your fellow so that the L-rd will be your G-d, through the offering of your self to G-d, in [the recital of the word] *Echad*, as has been discussed above.

---

51. *Chagigah* 5b; *Kallah*, beg. ch. 3; *Vayikrah Rabbah* 26:7.

52. Job 11:11.

53. Job 3:23.

54. A compilation of the Rabbi Yitzchak Luria's kabbalistic teachings, by his pri-

וְאֵין פֵּירוּשׁ לֹא הִבִּיט וְלֹא רָאָה שֶׁנֶּעֱלָמִים מִמֶּנּוּ חַס וְשָׁלוֹם כִּי הַכֹּל גָּלוּי וְיָדוּעַ וַאֲפִילוּ שִׂיחָה קַלָּה כוּ׳ אֶלָּא כְּמוֹ שֶׁכָּתוּב וַיֵּרָא אָוֶן וְלֹא יִתְבּוֹנָן (איוב י״א י״א) שֶׁאֵין נִמְשָׁךְ מִן הַיְדִיעָה שֶׁלּוֹ שֶׁיּוֹדֵעַ אוֹתָם בְּדַעְתּוֹ יִתְבָּרַךְ שֶׁאֵין לָהּ גְּבוּל וְתַכְלִית לִידֵי הִתְפַּעֲלוּת בְּמִדּוֹת הַגְּבוּרָה כוּ׳ כִּי הָאַהֲבָה תְּכַסֶּה וּכְמוֹ שֶׁכָּתוּב וַיָּסֶךְ אֱלוֹהַּ בַּעֲדוֹ (איוב ג׳ כ״ג) אֱלוֹהַּ הוּא אֵל ו"ה שֶׁהוּא חֶסֶד עֶלְיוֹן הַמַּקִּיף כְּמוֹ שֶׁכָּתוּב בְּעֵץ חַיִּים׳ (שֶׁהוּא לְבוּשׁ הַנְּשָׁמָה וְחוֹתְמָהּ עַיֵּן שָׁם)

מַה שֶּׁאֵין כֵּן אִם יֵשׁ פֵּירוּד חַס וְשָׁלוֹם בְּיִשְׂרָאֵל כָּל אֲשֶׁר בּוֹ מוּם לֹא יִקְרָב וְיִגְרְמוּ לְמַעְלָה בְּחִינַת פֵּירוּד וְאָז יִהְיֶה רוֹאֶה אֶת הַחוֹב וּבִפְרָט עָלָיו שֶׁהוּא הַמַּפְרִיד רַחֲמָנָא לִיצְלָן מִזֶּה

וּבְרָכֵנוּ אָבִינוּ כֻּלָּנוּ כְּאֶחָד וְאָז כֻּלָּךְ יָפָה רַעְיָתִי וּמוּם אֵין בָּךְ (שִׁיר הַשִּׁירִים ד׳ ז׳) וְנַעֲשָׂה בְּחִינַת יִחוּד קוּדְשָׁא בְּרִיךְ הוּא וּשְׁכִינְתֵּיהּ גִּלּוּי אוֹר אֵין סוֹף בִּמְקוֹר נִשְׁמוֹת יִשְׂרָאֵל לְמֶהֱוֵי אֶחָד בְּאֶחָד

וְזֶה סוֹד תָּמִים תִּהְיֶה[56] עִם ה׳ אֱלֹקֶיךָ (דְּבָרִים י"ח י"ג) כְּמוֹ שֶׁה׳ אֱלֹקֶיךָ הוּא עִם כְּלָלוּת נִשְׁמוֹת יִשְׂרָאֵל בְּחִינַת תָּם דְּהַיְינוּ הֶאָרַת חָכְמָה עִילָּאָה בִּכְלָלוּת אֵיבָרִים דִּשְׁכִינְתֵּיהּ וְאָהַבְתָּ לְרֵעֲךָ כָּמוֹךָ וְאֵין רוֹאֶה חוֹבוֹתָיו כְּמוֹ כֵן תִּהְיֶה אַתָּה תָּמִים עִם חֲבֵירֶיךָ כְּדֵי שֶׁיִּהְיֶה ה׳ אֱלֹקֶיךָ בִּמְסִירַת נֶפֶשׁ בְּאֶחָד כְּמוֹ שֶׁכָּתוּב לְעֵיל:

---

mary disciple and exponent, Rabbi Chaim Vital (1543 – 1620).

55. Song of Songs 4:7.

56. Deuteronomy 19:13.

This is why Hillel said "all the rest is but commentary." For, as is known, the purpose of all the *mitzvot* is to bring about the unity of the Holy One, blessed is He, with His *Shechinah*. Now, the essential unity of the Supernal Being with His *Shechinah*, called the *Beauty of Jacob*, depends upon the revelation of the true love, becoming actual self-love, for as mentioned above, "His people are part of G-d."

This is accomplished through the performance of the *mitzvah*, "You shall love your fellow as yourself," as explained above. All the other *mitzvot* are like a commentary that explains the unity.

(That is, in what form shall this unity take: whether an intellectual unity—man's wisdom with G-d's Wisdom—through Torah study, or an emotional unity of love or the other emotional attributes through the performance of the other *mitzvot*. As for example, if a person forms a strong bond of friendship with another, the cause of the attachment is true love.

## MITZVOT

The close relationship can take various forms: at times in speech, conversing upon intellectual matters; at times in emotion, displaying love for him; at times in deed, in doing him favors. Likewise, the 248 positive *mitzvot* correspond to the "248 organs of the King."[57] The performance of a specific *mitzvah* brings about the unity intrinsic to the particular organ [to which the *mitzvah* corresponds] and all the other attributes are contained within it. The same is the case in the performance of all other *mitzvot*).

For example, the *mitzvah* of wrapping oneself in the *tallit* [whose aim is to] "Accept upon yourself a King,"[58] [drawing over himself] the encompassing Light. This enables the recipient to offer his soul to G-d in [the recital of the word] *Echad*. For "if there is no fear [of G-d], there is no wisdom."[59] The fear which follows wisdom—as it is written, "If there is no wisdom there is no fear"—is complete self-abnegation which comes because of one's closeness to G-d. For the characteristic of fear is that as one comes closer, one is more overcome with a feeling of awe. The characteristic of love, on

---

57. *Tikkunei Zohar, Tikun* 30. V. *Tanya*, Part 1, ch. 23.

58. Deuteronomy 17, 15; See *Tanya*, Part 1, ch. 41.

TRANSLATION AND COMMENTARY

וְזֶהוּ שֶׁאָמַר הִלֵּל וְאִידָךְ פֵּירוּשָׁא הוּא שֶׁהֲרֵי כָּל הַמִּצְוֹת הֵם לְיַיחֵד קוּדְשָׁא בְּרִיךְ הוּא וּשְׁכִינְתֵּיהּ כַּיָדוּעַ וַהֲרֵי עִיקַר הַיִּחוּד אָדָם דִּלְעֵילָא בִּשְׁכִינְתֵּיהּ הַנִּקְרֵאת שׁוּפְרֵיהּ דְּיַעֲקֹב הוּא תָּלוּי בְּהִתְגַּלּוּת הָאַהֲבָה אֲמִיתִּית עַד לִהְיוֹת כָּמוֹךְ מַמָּשׁ חֵלֶק ה' עַמּוֹ כַּנַ"ל,

וְזֶה נַעֲשֶׂה עַל יְדֵי קִיּוּם מִצְוַת וְאָהַבְתָּ לְרֵעֲךָ כָּמוֹךָ כַּנַ"ל וּשְׁאָר כָּל הַמִּצְוֹת הֵם כְּמוֹ פֵּירוּשׁ לְהַסְבִּיר הַיִּחוּד

(דְּהַיְינוּ בְּאֵיזוֹ אוֹפֶן יִהְיֶה הַיִּחוּד אִם חָכְמָתוֹ בְּחָכְמָתוֹ בְּתַלְמוּד תּוֹרָה וְאַהֲבָה בְּאַהֲבָה וּשְׁאָרֵי מִדּוֹת עַל יְדֵי שְׁאָרֵי מִצְוֹת וּכְמוֹ שֶׁבָּאָדָם הַמִּתְדַּבֵּק וּמִתְקַשֵּׁר עִם חֲבֵירוֹ סִיבַּת הַהִתְקַשְּׁרוּת הוּא הָאַהֲבָה הָאֲמִיתִּית

וְהַיִּחוּד פְּעָמִים בְּדִבּוּר שֶׁמְּדַבֵּר עִמּוֹ דִּבְרֵי חָכְמָה וּפְעָמִים בְּמִדּוֹת בְּהִתְגַּלּוּת אַהֲבָתוֹ לוֹ וּפְעָמִים בְּמַעֲשֶׂה בְּטוֹבוֹת גַּשְׁמִיּוֹת וְכָךְ יֵשׁ רַמַ"ח מִצְוֹת עֲשֵׂה הֵם רַמַ"ח אֵיבָרִים דְּמַלְכָּא וּבְמִצְוָה זוֹ עִיקַר הַיִּחוּד בְּאֵבֶר זֶה וּשְׁאָר הַבְּחִינוֹת כְּלוּלִים בּוֹ וְכֵן עַל דֶּרֶךְ זֶה בִּשְׁאָר כָּל הַמִּצְוֹת)

כְּמוֹ מִצְוַת עֲטִיפַת הַטַּלִּית שׂוֹם תָּשִׂים עָלֶיךָ מֶלֶךְ (דְּבָרִים י"ז ט"ו) בְּחִינַת אוֹר מַקִּיף שֶׁיִּהְיֶה כֹּחַ לְהַמְקַבֵּל לִמְסוֹר נַפְשׁוֹ בְּאֶחָד כִּי אִם אֵין יִרְאָה אֵין חָכְמָה (אָבוֹת פֶּרֶק ג' מִשְׁנָה י"ז)[59] וְהַיִּרְאָה שֶׁאַחַר הַחָכְמָה וּכְמוֹ שֶׁכָּתוּב אִם אֵין חָכְמָה אֵין יִרְאָה הַיְינוּ בִּיטוּל בִּמְצִיאוּת מִפְּנֵי הַקֵּירוּב כִּי מִדַּת הַיִּרְאָה הִיא כָּל

---

59. *Avot* 3:7.

the other hand, is that the further one moves [from the object of his love], the stronger the love grows.

RESULT

Accordingly, after a person has grasped the concept of His Oneness, he will be instilled with an awe of total self-surrender. And the vestige thereof becomes invested in the encompassing aspect of the *tallit*, inspiring him with an external fear that precedes wisdom.

All this is only an explanation of the unity generated by the soul's faculty of wisdom, when one offers his soul to G-d through [the recital of the word] *Echad*. This is the deeper meaning of unity, which essentially derives from the positive *mitzvah* of "Love your fellow..." For then, "*You are altogether beautiful, My beloved,*" and "*You shall be perfect with the L-rd your G-d,*" as explained above.

ANOTHER PERSPECTIVE

This *mitzvah* of "You shall love," and especially the negative precept, "You shall not hate..." can be explained from another perspective. That is, in light of the exposition, elsewhere,[60] on the verse, "Choose from among you...to bring the L-rd's retribution upon Midian."[61] There it explains that the *kelipah*[62] of Midian is baseless hatred, and the retribution of G-d must be executed upon Midian. See there.

---

60. Rabbi Schneur Zalman of Liadi, *Likkutei Torah*, *Matot*, 85d ff. [See also *On Ahavat Yisrael*, Kehot.]

61. Numbers 31:3.

62. *Kelipah*, or "shell" is the symbol fre-

הַקְרֵב קָרֵב יוֹתֵר, יוֹתֵר תִּפּוֹל עָלָיו הַבִּטּוּל מַה שֶּׁאֵין כֵּן הָאַהֲבָה מֵרָחוֹק תִּתְגַּבֵּר יוֹתֵר

וְלָכֵן אַחַר הַחָכְמָה בְּאֶחָד תִּהְיֶה הַיִּרְאָה בִּטּוּל בִּמְצִיאוּת, וּנְקֻדַּת הָרְשִׁימוּ מִמֶּנָּה יִתְלַבֵּשׁ בְּהַמַּקִּיף שֶׁל הַטַּלִּית הַיִּרְאָה שֶׁמִּבַּחוּץ שֶׁקּוֹדֶם לַחָכְמָה

וְכָל זֶה רַק פֵּירוּשׁ לְהַיִּחוּד שֶׁהוּא בְּחָכְמָה שֶׁבַּנֶּפֶשׁ כְּשֶׁמּוֹסֵר נַפְשׁוֹ בְּאֶחָד שֶׁזֶּה סוֹד הַיִּחוּד שֶׁעִיקָרוֹ הוּא עַל יְדֵי מִצְוֹת עֲשֵׂה דְוְאָהַבְתָּ שֶׁאָז כֻּלָּךְ יָפָה רַעְיָתִי וְתָמִים תִּהְיֶה עִם ה׳ אֱלֹקֶיךָ וּכְמוֹ שֶׁנִּתְבָּאֵר לְמַעְלָה:

וְעוֹד יֵשׁ לְבָאֵר טַעַם טוֹב לְמִצְוָה זוֹ דְוְאָהַבְתָּ לְרֵעֲךָ כָּמוֹךָ וּבִפְרָט לְלֹא תַעֲשֶׂה דְלֹא תִשְׂנָא כוּ׳ עַל פִּי מַה שֶּׁכָּתוּב בְּמָקוֹם אַחֵר בַּפָּסוּק הֵחָלְצוּ מֵאִתְּכֶם' כוּ׳ לָתֵת נִקְמַת ה׳ בְּמִדְיָן (בַּמִּדְבָּר ל"א ג׳) שֶׁקְּלִיפַת מִדְיָן הוּא שִׂנְאַת חִנָּם וְצָרִיךְ לִהְיוֹת נִקְמַת הוי׳ בְּמִדְיָן יְעוּיַּן שָׁם:

---

quently used in Kabbalah to denote "evil" and the source of sensual desires in human nature.

# HEBREW NOTES

# HEBREW NOTES

## הערות כ"ק אדמו"ר זי"ע למצות אהבת ישראל
(כפי שנדפסו בקונטרס "אהבת ישראל" – קה"ת תשל"ו).

א. תניא פל"ב. לקו"ת ס"פ מטות. (כנראה הוא הנסמן בסוף מצוה זו).

ב. נתלים בראשו מהם בזרועו כו': ואולי י"ל דנקט רישא וסיפא דמרז"ל תנחומא תשא יב – שהוזכר בש' הפוסקים בראשית ד"ג.

ג. נק' אדם אדמה לעליון: ראה של"ה חלק תורה שבכתב וישב סוף הדרוש צאן יוסף ובכ"מ. גם בס' עשרה מאמרות אם כל חי חלק ב' פל"ג ועוד.

ד. שהם קומה שלימה: ראה לקו"ת ר"פ נצבים. ובכ"מ.

ה. ולכן נצטוינו ג"כ לאהוב כל אדם מישראל שהרי .. בו יש זולתו .. עצמו ובשרו הוא: ראה ירושלמי נדרים פ"ט ה"ד: הוה מקטע קופד ואחת סכתא לידוי תחזור ותמחי לידי' (בתמי').

ו. שלימה ובריאה: להעיר ממאגה"ק סל"א.

ז. כמ"ש בע"ח: ראה ש' מ"ן ומ"ד ד"ח. לקוט שמע"צ פט, ב. וראה הגהות הצ"צ לתניא רפ"ב. מאו"א בערכו.

ח. תמים תהי': ראה לקו"ת נצבים מה, ג. אוה"ת שם.

ט. ונדודות .. הטלית: ראה לקו"ת ס"פ שלח ור"פ קורח.

י. מ"ש .. החלצו מאתכם: לקו"ת ס"פ מטות. ועייג"כ החלצו רנ"ט. ובכ"מ.

## BRIEF BIOGRAPHY

## BRIEF BIOGRAPHY OF
## RABBI MENACHEM MENDEL OF LUBAVITCH
## 5549–5626 (1789–1866)

Rabbi Menachem Mendel was born on Erev Rosh Hashanah 5549 (1789). His mother, Devorah Leah (daughter of Rabbi Schneur Zalman of Liadi), passed away three days after his third birthday, and from that day the young orphan was reared and educated by his famous grandfather.

The young lad's prodigious abilities became evident early on. By the time he was twelve he had written many treatises on matters of Halachic importance and had begun recording the Talmudic and Chasidic teachings of his grandfather, supplementing them with his own comments and explanations.

While still in his teens, he was appointed by Rabbi Schneur Zalman to engage in the necessary research and reply to the numerous Halachic enquiries pouring in from scholars in Russia and Europe.

When Rabbi Menachem Mendel was only eighteen years old, the manuscript of his famous Chasidic discourse, *Shoresh Mitzvat Hatefillah*, which he had tried to conceal, was discovered by his grandfather. Rabbi Schneur Zalman was so delighted with his find that he thereafter allotted more time for their study together.

Rabbi Menachem Mendel was only twenty when he was appointed to take charge of most of Rabbi Schneur Zalman's communal affairs.

After the passing of Rabbi Schneur Zalman in 5573 (1812), Rabbi DovBer (the father-in-law of Rabbi Menachem Mendel) was appointed his successor. At this time Rabbi Menachem Mendel commenced a period of fourteen years of seclusion, during which he devoted himself to study and prayer. He emerged to play his part in public life in 5587 (1826), at the time when Rabbi DovBer was accused of subversive activities. His first activity was the organization of a committee to defend Rabbi DovBer.

When Rabbi DovBer died in 5588 (1827), the chasidim, in recognition of Rabbi Menachem Mendel's outstanding abilities, called on him to accept the leadership of the Chabad-Lubavitch movement. For many months he rejected the tremendous responsibility of this position, but finally, he reluctantly answered the call.

Rabbi Menachem Mendel was a prolific writer. His works contain a unique synthesis of the hidden and the manifest in which Talmudic, Midrashic, Kabbalistic and Chasidic thought are harmoniously and lucidly blended.

He would certainly have liked nothing better than to continue his writings, edit the works of his grandfather and father-in-law, and lead the countless chasidim who had swelled the ranks of Lubavitch. But this era had its own share of problems with which Jews were confronted.

Jews in Russia were barred from most occupations and business opportunities, and poverty was rampant among them. Deeply interested in the economic position of the Jewish people, Rabbi Menachem Mendel advised the chasidim to engage in agriculture wherever possible, and he gave financial aid to those who followed his advice.

At that time it was the policy of the Russian Government to make it difficult for Jews to settle in the villages, so Rabbi Menachem Mendel bought a large tract of land near the city of Minsk on which to settle many Jewish families. In 5604 (1844) he bought another large area of land with some adjoining forests in Minsk Province from Prince Shzedrinov, and established the settlement of Shzedrin. A council was organized to direct its affairs.

The founding of Shzedrin made a deep impression on Jews and non-Jews. In a government report from the official of the Province of Minsk to the Minister of Interior, they spoke of Rabbi Schneersohn of Lubavitch with respect and praise.

The report mentioned that he had acquired a large tract of land and established there a settlement for Jews, thereby raising their living conditions and improving their position. It also spoke of the great influence of the Rabbi of Lubavitch on all the Jews living within the pale of the Russian Empire and of the manner in which he constantly tried to improve their material living conditions.

In the year 5587 (1827) Czar Nicholas I instituted the "Cantonist" edict, which introduced the conscription of children for military training and service. Originally it applied to children of the age of twelve years old and older. The Jewish communities had to supply a quota of ten children per thousand (non-Jews had a smaller quota and more liberal exemptions).

The children were sent away by government officials and distributed among the peasantry, or sent to special schools until the age of eighteen. They were then removed to barracks for military service for twenty-five years.

This meant that the children were torn from home and from *cheder* for the greater part of their lives, and were subjected to treatment calculated to estrange them from their own people.

No parent would willingly yield a child for such a callous scheme, but the community was obliged to provide its quota, so the children had to be taken by force. This led to the appearance of a despicable character, the "snatcher," whose job was to catch or kidnap the children and hand them over to the government officials. Heart-breaking scenes, with children being torn from their mothers' arms, became common occurrences. The brunt of the tragedy fell upon the poorer Jews, who were unable to buy their children's freedom from the snatchers.

Rabbi Menachem Mendel attacked the problem without regard to the dangers involved. It was necessary to save as many as possible of the children who were actually conscripted. To this end Rabbi Menachem Mendel organized a special council for the following three purposes:

First, to study the position of the individual Jewish communities, with a view to helping them decrease the number of children they would have to supply.

Secondly, to engage in freeing those who had been captured. It was arranged to achieve this through the organization of a special clandestine society known as "Techiat Hameitim" (the "Resurrection of the Dead").

The method employed was to pay a ransom for each child to the officials concerned. They would return the child, at the same time reporting to the authorities that the child in question had died during the journey. They would also officially inform the community concerned of the "death" of the child. These "death certificates" brought great happiness to the parents.

Obviously, the children had to be hidden for a long time. Those who were saved were called members of the Techiat Hameitim society. They were then sent to *chadorim* or Talmud Torahs far from their home towns.

Thirdly, to send special trustworthy people to the places where the cantonist children were stationed to encourage and urge them to remain faithful to their religion and to their people.

Apart form the huge expense it involved, this responsible work was highly dangerous, for it amounted to an act of treason. Yet this underground program was successfully carried out and was never betrayed.

At the same time, Rabbi Menachem Mendel concentrated his efforts on supporting the agricultural centers in the districts of Vitebsk and Minsk. He dispatched Rabbi Hillel of Paritch, one of the leading chasidim, to the settlements in the district of Kherson, where he spent several months each summer.

Besides instructing the Jews there in the study of the Torah and the fear of G-d in accordance with Chasidic teachings, he inspired them to rise to a high level of brotherly love, mutual help and generally high moral conduct.

During the twelve years from 5587 to 5599 (1827-1839), Rabbi Menachem Mendel concentrated his efforts on communal activities in the field of material aid; the protection of Jewish children from the kidnappers and their maintenance in safety, and spiritual help for the cantonists.

Rabbi Menachem Mendel devoted particular attention to the requirements of the Jewish conscripts in the Russian army. He ensured that there should be special representatives at every place where Jewish troops were stationed, with the specific aim of concerning themselves with the troops' moral conduct. These representatives were to encourage the soldiers and strengthen them from falling into the traps of conversion laid for them by eager missionaries.

Rabbi Menachem Mendel also worked for the support of needy Torah scholars studying at the *yeshivot* and advanced institutes of learning.

During all these years he carried on his work without any interference from the opponents of chasidism in either the religious or the so-called "enlightened" groups in Russia. During this time also, there was no conflict between chasidim and *mitnagdim*. On Rabbi Menachem Mendel's frequent visits to chasidic communities in Minsk and Vilna, the *mitnagdim* always accorded him great honor and attended his Chasidic and Talmudic discourses.

In 5603 (1843) the Russian Government announced that a conference was to be held at S. Petersburg for the purpose of deciding important religious problems. It was the intention of the government, at the instigation of the *maskilim*, to use the conference as a means to introduce into the school system innovations which would interfere with traditional procedures in Jewish education and prayer.

A Rabbinical Commission composed of leaders of chasidim and *mitnagdim* was convened to plan how best to combat the threat the conference posed. Rabbi Menachem Mendel was appointed to the Commission.

The first meeting between Rabbi Menachem Mendel and Rabbi

Yitzchak of Volozhin, the leader of the *mitnagdim*, made a favorable impression on both of them. Observers remarked that the meeting proved to the *mitnagdim* that the chasidim were scholars, and convinced the chasidim that the *mitnagdim* were pious.

This rapprochement and communal cooperation had salutary effects on the general relationship between chasidim and *mitnagdim*. The antagonists were reunited and began to work together for the common cause of traditional Judaism.

At the first meeting of the conference, Rabbi Menachem Mendel expressed his opinion that the purpose of the conference could only be to encourage religious observance among the Jews and he reiterated the indefensibility of tampering even with Jewish custom, since customs are also considered Torah. Despite threats by the chairman of the conference, a Minister of Government, and being placed under house arrest on numerous occasions during the four-month period of the conference, Rabbi Menachem Mendel showed unswerving determination to oppose any proposed change of any Jewish custom whatsoever.

"We are not summoned to legislate," he said. "We are here to clarify statutes previously decided in the laws of the Mosaic faith. We are here to clarify too, the customs of Israel, to protect both the commandments of G-d and Jewish usage from tampering."

The conference ended without the adoption of any of the changes proposed by the *maskilim*. Rabbi Menachem Mendel's resoluteness and selflessness impressed all the participants and enhanced his already considerable reputation.

The granting of honorary citizenship papers signed by Czar Nicholas was one of the honors bestowed on Rabbi Menachem Mendel in 5604 (1844), in recognition of his valuable work at the S. Petersburg conference the previous year.

This great honor bestowed on Rabbi Menachem Mendel by the government made a deep impression on the Jewish population throughout the Russian Empire. Whenever an important problem arose concerning the Jewish community in White Russia, Rabbi Menachem Mendel was consulted and asked to negotiate with the government. The communal activities of Rabbi Menachem Mendel thus spread into even wider fields.

He made every effort to improve the economic conditions of the Jews in the Pale of Settlement. Of all the inhabitants of Russia, only the Jews were discriminated against in the matter of where they could live. They were allowed to settle only in certain districts forming a belt or pale, hence the Pale of Settlement. Even there, they were restricted to the urban areas and kept out of the rural areas.

At the conclusion of the Rabbinical conference, Rabbi Menachem Mendel submitted a report to the Minister of the Interior on the economic situation of the Jews in the Pale of Settlement, and petitioned the Government to extend it.

The reaction of the Minister of the Interior was favorable, and at the suggestion of one of his assistants, he invited Rabbi Menachem Mendel, together with two interpreters Mr. Feitelson and Mr. Chaikin to come and see him in the capital in order to elaborate on his proposals. The Minsiter received Rabbi Menachem Mendel courteously and assured him that his proposals would be submitted to the next session of the Cabinet.

Several days later, one of the assistants of the Minister of the Interior announced that, although Rabbi Schneersohn's proposals concerning the economic plight of the Jews in the Provinces of Vitebsk, Mohilev and Minsk had not been accepted in full, a decree had been issued forbidding the expulsion of Jews from villages and estates if they were already settled there. The precarious position of many Jews was thus legalized, and the Pale was in fact extended.

News of the new regulation gained by Rabbi Menachem Mendel spread among the Jews, and hundreds of Jewish families took advantage of the new development to infiltrate into the new zone, finding ways to antedate their move so that it would meet the requirements of the law.

During the summer of 5604 (1844), several hundred families settled on the land and earned a good livelihood. Furthermore, as a result of the exodus from the cities, the problems of overcrowding and competition were eased.

Rabbi Menachem Mendel's personal magnetism drew tens of thousands of chasidim from all parts of Europe and Russia, and his thirty-eight years as leader of the movement were a colorful and flourishing period for Chabad. His efforts, like those of his predecessors, served as an inspiration to his son Rabbi Shmuel, who succeeded his father upon his passing on 13 Nissan 5626 (1866).

# IMPORTANT DATES

## IMPORTANT DATES IN THE LIFE OF
## RABBI MENACHEM MENDEL

5549 (1789): Birth of Rabbi Menachem Mendel, the Tzemach Tzedek, on Erev Rosh Hashanah.

5562 (1802): Begins recording novellae in Talmud and Chasidus that he heard from his grandfather, Rabbi Schneur Zalman, and his own novellae in explaining these subjects.

5563 (1803): His marriage to Rebbetzin Chaya Mushka.

5566 (1806): Rabbi Schneur Zalman assigns him, and his great-uncle Rabbi Yehuda Leib, the responsibility of responding to questions on Torah law.

5569 (1809): Accompanies Rabbi Schneur Zalman to Volhynia.

5570 (1810): Rabbi Schneur Zalman charges him and his uncle Rabbi Moshe, (Rabbi Schneur Zalman's son) with involvement in communal matters.

5574-87 (1814-27): Isolates himself and studies Torah with extraordinary diligence.

5588 (1828): Accepts the post of Rebbe. From the beginning of the period of military conscription for Jews, the period of the "snatchers" (child-kidnappers for the army) and the Cantonists, 5587-5615 (1827-1855), he totally dedicates himself and rescues scores of thousands of young conscripts from apostasy and death.

5597 (1837): Publishes Rabbi Schneur Zalman's *Torah Or*.

5598 (1838): Travels through Mogilev and Minsk provinces to Vilna, returning via Vitebsk province.
5599 (1839): Aquires the Schtzedrin tract of land from Price

Schtzedrinov in Minsk province, with forest and farmland and establishes the Schtzedrin (Shidrin) colony, giving land and agricultural implements to Jewish farmer-settlers.

5600 (1840): Is accused by the community K. of opposing the community's procedures in handing over Jewish children for conscription. Mordechai Aaron G's accusation in the name of the *maskilim* of Vilna and Volhynia.

5601 (1841): Is slandered by two "snatchers" from Borisov.

5602 (1842): Receives "Honored Citizens" award signed by the Czar.

5603 (1843): Is requested to participate in the Rabbinical Commision in Petersberg. For his protest against the *maskilim* of Vilna and Riga, his demand that the publication of sacred books be permitted, and his protest against the prohibition of publishing works of Chasidus and Kabbalah—he is arrested numerous times during the course of the Commision. His demands are fulfilled.

5605 (1845): Receives "Honored Citizen for Posterity" award.

5608 (1848): Publishes Rabbi Schneur Zalman's *Likkutei Torah*.

5614 (1854): Protests the Ministry's demand, as proposed by Dr. Max Lilienthal, to abridge the *Siddur* for children and to institute the abridged *Chumash* for children.

5616 (1856): A fire destroys his home and five chests of manuscripts.

5621 (1861): Widowed on the eighth of Tevet.

5626 (1866): Passes away on Wednesday night, the eve of Nissan 13, and is interred in Lubavitch.

His sons:
1) Rabbi Baruch Shalom.
2) Rabbi Yehuda Leib.
3) Rabbi Chaim Schneur Zalman.
4) Rabbi Yisrael Noach.
5) Rabbi Yosef Yitzchak.
6) Rabbi Yaakov.
7) Rabbi Shmuel.

His daughters:
1) Rebbetzin Rada Freida; married Rabbi Schneur.
2) Rebbetzin Devorah Leah; married Rabbi Levi Yitzchak.

# PUBLISHED WORKS

## PUBLISHED WORKS OF RABBI MENACHEM MENDEL

1. *Derech Mitzvotecha (Sefer Hamitzvot).*
2. *Derech Emunah (Sefer Hachakira).*
3. *Or Hatorah, 42 vol:*
   *Bereishit – 7 vol.*
   *Shemot – 8 vol.*
   *Vayikra – 4 vol.*
   *Bamidbar – 6 vol.*
   *Devarim – 7 vol.*
   *Prophets and Writings – 3 vol.*
   *Tehillim (Yahel Or) – 1 vol.*
   *Megillat Esther – 1 vol.*
   *Shir Hashirim – 3 vol.*
   *Maamari Razal V'Inyanim – 1 vol.*
   *Siddur (Tefillah) – 1 vol.*
4. *Tzemach Tzedek Responsa, Novellae on Mishna, Halachic decisions – 8 vol.*
5. *Kitzurim V'ha'arot L'sefer Likkutei Amarim Tanya.*
6. *Biurei Hazohar – 2 vol.*
7. *Sefer Halikutim – Dach Tzemach Tzedek, 27 vol.*
8. *Kuntres Maamarim Al Maamarei Chazal B'Masechtot Bava Metzia u'Bava Batra.*
9. *Maamar U'she'avtem Mayim.*
10. *Igrot Kodesh, 2 vol.*
11. *Maamarei Admor Hatzemach Tzedek, 5614 – 5615.*

### *English Translations:*
12. *Mitzvat Ahavat Yisrael.*

# APPENDIX
## TWO STORIES

## LOVING-KINDNESS

### I.

Reb Yisrael lived in Polotsk. He was a simple merchant who spent his day managing a small shop which generated a humble income. Reb Yisrael could not boast of any great accomplishments, especially when it concerned his Torah knowledge. His simple mind could grasp elementary, uncomplicated texts and little more.

One year, a few weeks after the month of *Tishrei*, Reb Yisrael traveled to Lubavitch, to Rabbi Menachem Mendel. The Torah portion of that week was *Vayera*, and the Rebbe's discourse centered on the kindheartedness of the Patriarch Abraham and his charitable deeds.

In his discourse, the Rebbe cited a remark found in kabbalistic works. "The Attribute of Kindness complained before G-d," quoted the Rebbe. "It said, 'Ever since Abraham began his deeds, I have little work left to do.'"

Rabbi Menachem Mendel then elaborated on this idea, explaining that Abraham's physical deeds of kindness had simply replaced the selfsame spiritual attribute. In effect, Abraham stood spiritually higher than this spiritual virtue of Kindness: had this attribute descended into this material realm it could not have channeled kindness into the physical sphere. Abraham, however, was capable of this feat, due to the unique powers granted to the soul to facilitate its mission and elevate the material world.

Reb Yisrael, simple merchant that he was, did not grasp most of the Chassidic discourse. He did, however, understand certain words, and the Rebbe's remark about acts of kindness had particularly caught his ear. He repeated these words to himself, reviewing them until they permeated his essence.

Reb Yisrael returned home and, as was the custom, the local chasidim hosted a festive reception to celebrate his visit to the Rebbe. They gathered around the simple shopkeeper, pressing for details about his trip. "Maybe you can review the discourse you heard?' they asked.

"No," said Reb Yisrael. "I only know a few words; the rest was too difficult for me." He then repeated the phrases he had heard emphasizing the value of charitable deeds. The crowd listened carefully, thirstily absorbing the new teaching. When he finished, his friends dispersed to their respective schedules.

Reb Yisrael later went to resume his business in the marketplace, but the words of Rabbi Menachem Mendel reverberated in his ears, giving him no peace of mind. He reviewed the words again, trying to find its practical application in his everyday life. He did not need profound dissertations to affect his service of G-d; a few words from the Rebbe were enough.

It did not take long for the storekeeper to devise a plan. According to the Rebbe, physical charity had its merits over the corresponding spiritual attribute of kindness. He, the simple Yisrael, would do all he could to increase his personal charitable deeds and those of his acquaintances, Reb Nacham and Reb Yosef, shopkeepers like himself.

Reb Yisrael walked into the shop of Reb Nachman. "Give me a loan," he said, though he had no need for the money. "I just heard the most remarkable things from the Rebbe about the importance of charity. Since giving loans is one of the highest forms of charity, I propose we keep giving loans to each other. I will enable you to practice this good deed; later you do the same for me."

Reb Nachman readily agreed. He took a few coins and slid them over the counter to his friend. "What a marvelous idea!" he said excitedly. "Let's ask Yosef the merchant to join us."

And so it began. The three simple merchants—Yisrael, Nachman and Yosef—lent each other money on a daily basis. These free-loans became an integral part of their daily activities, and the threesome found gratification in fulfilling the Rebbe's words.

Months later, a curious thing happened when Reb Yisrael next arrived in Lubavitch. Rabbi Menachem Mendel himself exited his room and came into the synagogue, asking his attendant for the whereabouts of "Yisrael the shopkeeper." The attendant could proffer no help: Reb Yisrael kept to himself, very few chassidim knew his true worth, and the attendant simply had no idea who the Rebbe wanted.

Rabbi Menachem Mendel then turned to Chaim Ber, another attendant. "Who is this shopkeeper?" he demanded.

"You must mean Yisrael the shopkeeper from Polotsk," answered the attendant.

"Send him to me," instructed Rabbi Menachem Mendel.

The attendant quickly searched for the storekeeper and promptly sent him into the Rebbe's room. "What is your daily schedule?" the Rebbe asked as he entered the *yechidut* room.

"I rise at five in the morning," began Reb Yisrael. "I recite Psalms, have a cup of tea, prepare some firewood, and then I go to the synagogue to pray. Afterwards, I learn some *Mishnayot* before returning home to eat breakfast and beginning my day at the marketplace."

"I then go back to the synagogue after I finish working," continued the storekeeper. "I *daven mincha* and join a class in *Ein Yaakov*. After the evening prayers, I return home for the night.

"*Nu?*" prompted Rabbi Menachem Mendel. "And what about giving charity?"

Reb Yisrael shifted uneasily. "I'm a poor man," he said. "I have nothing to give."

Rabbi Menachem Mendel did not desist. He continued asking and prodding until the chasid explained his daily routine of giving and receiving free-loans with his friends. Satisfied with the reply, Rabbi Menachem Mendel wished his chasid well and ended the *yechidus*.

Later, Rabbi Menachem Mendel's son, Rabbi Shmuel asked his father about the extended *yechidus* granted to Reb Yisrael. "What did you see so special about him?" asked Reb Shmuel.

"I saw a pillar of heavenly fire rising above the head of this simple Reb Yisrael," said Rabbi Menachem Mendel. "I saw the Attribute of Kindness emanating from the supernal world of *Atzilut* shine brightly above this storekeeper."

## II.

Though his grandfather—the saintly Rabbi Schneur Zalman—had passed away many years earlier, Rabbi Menachem Mendel merited envisioning his grandfather often. At times he saw the Alter Rebbe at night; at times by day. This afforded him the unique opportunity to present his questions in Torah before his grandfather for solution. With time, Rabbi Menachem Mendel prepared for these visions by accumulating his questions in advance.

Rabbi Menachem Mendel was therefore quite distressed when these visions suddenly ceased. It was 5575 (1815), and Rabbi Menachem Mendel had gathered many complex Torah questions for which he could find no answer. He had always relied on his grandfather for answers and felt greatly anguished at this sudden change.

As Rabbi Menachem Mendel went to synagogue one morning, he passed through the village marketplace and was approached by one of the merchants, a chasid by the name of Mordechai Eliyahu. "Could you lend me five or six rubles just until tonight?" he asked Rabbi Menachem Mendel. "I expect to make a profit during market hours today."

"Certainly," replied Rabbi Menachem Mendel. "Come to my house after I return from the synagogue and I will loan you whatever you need."

As Rabbi Menachem Mendel arrived at the synagogue, a certain Talmudic teaching occurred to him. "Rabbi Elazar gave a coin to the poor and subsequently prayed (*Bava Batra* 10a)" he thought. "The Talmud (*Succah* 49b) also states that loaning money is greater than charity."

Rabbi Menachem Mendel immediately regretted his actions. Rather than delaying the good deed, he should have offered Mordechai Eliyahu the loan immediately. Closing his prayer book, Rabbi Menachem Mendel left the synagogue, returned home, and took out the amount of money the merchant needed.

Rabbi Menachem Mendel could hear a loud commotion as he retraced his steps to the marketplace. Dozens of merchants had descended on the market place, each offering various kinds of wares. Customers haggled loudly, animals brayed, clucked and mooed, and merchants fought with each other over prospective customers. Finding Mordechai Eliyahu now would be no easy task.

Rabbi Menachem Mendel walked slowly through the bustling marketplace, looking intently at every face. The minutes ticked away as he sought out the needy merchant. Finally, after much effort, the Rebbe located Reb Mordechai Eliyahu and gave the grateful merchant the funds he so desperately needed.

Leaving the busy market behind, Rabbi Menachem Mendel returned to the synagogue to resume his prayers. A pleasant surprise awaited him: hardly had Rabbi Menachem Mendel donned his *tallit* and *tefillin* when the Alter Rebbe suddenly appeared before him, his face radiating spiritual joy. "Loaning money to a fellow Jew in a wholehearted fashion has great merit," said the Alter Rebbe. "Doing a favor for a fellow Jew without imposing restriction, in accordance with the great precept to 'Love your fellow as yourself,' throws the portals of Heaven wide open."

Rabbi Menachem Mendel realized he had merited this divine revelation in merit of loaning charity before starting his own prayers. He then advanced his complex questions, receiving the Alter Rebbe's replies for all his queries.

Decades later, when he related this incident to his son and successor Rabbi Shmuel, Rabbi Menachem Mendel added the following: "Helping another Jew earn his livelihood—even just to earn seventy *kopeks* on a calf—opens the doors of all the Heavenly chambers."

*(Sefer Hasichot 5701, pp. 44-45;*
*Igrot Kodesh of Rabbi Yosef Yitzchak, vol. 4, pp. 522-523;*
*Sefer Hasichot 5701, pp. 97-99.*
*See also HaYom Yom, 28 Sivan;*
*Bati L'gani 5711 (Sefer Hamaamarim Melukat p. 8))*

# APPENDIX

## EXCERPTS FROM
## SEFER HA'ARACHIM–CHABAD
## MITZVAT AHAVAT YISRAEL

# EXCERPTS FROM
## SEFER HA'ARACHIM–CHABAD
## MITZVAT AHAVAT YISRAEL

DEFINITION

The *mitzvah* of *ahavat Yisrael*[2] obligates us to love every Jew, not only because he possesses virtues, a keen intellect or fine character traits, but because he is a Jew.[3] As such, *ahavat Yisrael* is predicated upon the soul of a Jew.

The love for another should be akin to the love for oneself, as it says,[4] "And you shall love your friend as yourself"—exactly "as yourself." Meaning, a person's love for his fellow Jew must be an intrinsic love, a love that transcends logic, just as—and identical to—one's own self-love. If one's own personal affairs are of greater concern, then one has not yet achieved true *ahavat Yisrael*.

Moreover, a person must cherish the other even more than himself;[5] the needs of the other should concern him more; and the suffering of the other ought to be more distressing—may Heaven protect us. For a person can find justification for his own misfortunes, but to do so for someone else—is absolutely impossible.[6]

To attain such love requires profound reflection. Such reflection, though, serves only as a means to uncover this innate love, a love that surpasses the very understanding that reveals it. For *ahavat Yisrael* is a natural love, (not unlike the love between brothers, or the love of a father for his son,) which is engraved on every facet[7] of the soul.[8] The task, therefore, is to awaken this love.

THE RATIONALE FOR *AHAVAT YISRAEL*

Since people are distinct individuals, we would think that their love

---

1. Rambam, *Sefer HaMitvot*, command no. 206; Rambam, *Hilchot Dayot*, ch. 6, par. 3; *Chinuch*, command no. 243.
2. See *Kuntres Ahavat Yisrael*, (Kehot) sect. 4, where it is explained that there must also be a love that is based on the other person's particular virtues.
3. *Lev.* 19:18.
4. *HaYom Yom*, p. 26.
5. Hence, the true explanation of "love your friend as yourself" is not that one is bound to love one's friend as oneself. On the contrary, one is required to love *oneself* to the same extent that one loves another.

would be based on logic, and limited by its constraints. In truth, though, *ahavat Yisrael* is innate—for the following reasons:

1. *Ahavat Yisrael* springs from a Jew's love of G-d, for one loves what his beloved loves.[9] Therefore, [since *ahavat HaShem* is innate to every Jew] *ahavat Yisrael* is [also] natural and innate to every Jew.

2. All Jews constitute particular components of a single whole, namely, the soul of Adam, which was fragmented subsequently into a multitude of particular souls. Thus, every particular soul comprises within it all other particular souls. Consequently, one's fellow Jew is incorporated, spiritually, within oneself. Furthermore, from the perspective of their essential root, all souls form a single essence. When a single essence is divided into numerous parts, each part contains the entire essence.[10] A person's love for his fellow Jew, therefore, is not a love for another, but rather a love for oneself.

ACHIEVING *AHAVAT YISRAEL*

Only by recognizing the primacy of the soul and the subordination of the body can one attain *ahavat Yisrael*. If a person regards his body as preeminent and his soul as ancillary, then he cannot possibly possess genuine *ahavat Yisrael*—only a conditional love, at best. For from a corporeal perspective, possessing disparate bodies, he and his friend are two distinct human beings. Thus for an essential love to exist between them is utterly impossible. Only he who despises and disdains his body [in and of itself] and who discerns the primacy of his soul, can possess genuine *ahavat Yisrael*, an essential and unconditional love.[11]

Furthermore, even when an individual considers his soul to be

---

6. [Lit. "on every Jew's *neshamah, ruach,* and *nefesh*." These refer to different levels or aspects of the soul. See *Tanya*, ch. 2, 3; *Midrash Rabbah* on Gen. 14:19.]
7. *HaYom Yom*, p. 49.
8. See *Kuntres Ahavat Yisrael*, sect. 6.
9. Consonant with the dictum of the Baal Shem Tov: An essence, when grasped in part, is grasped in its entirety.
10. For this reason, *ahavat Yisrael* is analogous to *milah* (circumcision). *Orlah* (foreskin) symbolizes attachment to materialism. The idea of *milah* (removing the *orlah*) is to sever one's attachment to materialistic matters (so that one's involvement in all mundane pursuits is superficial), and to bind oneself to G-d's blessed unity. Since *ahavat Yisrael* is feasible only when worldly concerns are incidental to a person—"his soul is primary and his body secondary," the underlying concept of *ahavat Yisrael* is similar to that of *milah*.
11. *HaYom Yom*, p. 25.

preeminent, he can still not experience an essential love if he is mindful of his own distinct existence, though it be, admittedly, a purely spiritual one. Only when one's entire ego (*yeshut*) has been nullified can the quality of essence be revealed in a person—the singular essence common to every Jew. Then, because of the manifestation of the soul's essence, an essential love can flourish.

Though only possible when arising from the quintessence of the soul, as explained above, nonetheless, *ahavat Yisrael* arouses and reveals the soul's essence by a person cultivating and demonstrating this love. By identifying with the other, and shedding one's autonomous limitations, the essence of the soul is revealed.

## TO EVERY JEW

One must love every Jew without exception, including one whom he has never met[12] (since an essential love applies even to a complete stranger), and one with whom, in a spiritual sense, he is utterly distant. Not only must one have *ahavat Yisrael* for a simple fellow, but one must possess the same love for an abject sinner as for a consummate *tzaddik*.[13]

Because *ahavat Yisrael* is an essential love, no distinctions are drawn between wicked and righteous. When a person perceives his own misdeeds, his self-love conceals them, as it says, "love masks all misdeeds."[14] The reason for this is because the love derives from the core of his soul, a level at which faults are of absolutely no consequence. So, too, with *ahavat Yisrael*, all of the other's vices, even those of the wicked, are veiled.

This is the meaning of what Hillel the Elder taught the convert: "What you detest, do not inflict upon your friend."[15] A person overlooks his own liabilities.[16] On the other hand, if another perceives his shortcomings as serious, then he is profoundly perturbed. So observing the dictum, "… do not inflict upon your friend," a person should ignore the other's failings and transgressions, because of his tremendous love for him.

---

12. *Sefer HaSichot 5700*, p. 117.
13. *Proverbs* 10:12.
14. *Shabbat* 31a.
15. Though aware of his shortcomings, he considers them utterly negligible; his faults are inundated and nullified by the immense love that conceal them.
16. *Avodah Zarah* 26b; *Shulchan Aruch, Choshen Mishpat*, sect. 425.

For this reason, the wording of the directive, "One should love an incorrigible sinner just as one does a consummate *tzaddik*," falls short in conveying the true nature of *ahavat Yisrael*. For the phrase, "... an incorrigible sinner just as one does a consummate *tzaddik*," implies that there are various ranks. (Yet even so, one must still love an incorrigible sinner—yet only in a manner that approximates one's love for a consummate *tzaddik*—*just as*.) In truth, however, from the vantage point of an essential love, the spiritual state of another Jew is altogether irrelevant.

For this reason, Rabbi Yosef Yitzchak Schneersohn of Lubavitch was accustomed to reaching out to *all* Jews, even to those about whom it says, "We precipitate their downfall, and do not come to their aid."[17] When questioned about his conduct, his apparent disregard for the law pertaining to such scoundrels, and his persistence in reaching out to them, he replied:[18]

> The *Shulchan Aruch* comprises four volumes, of which *Choshen Mishpat* is the *fourth*. In this volume itself, there are over 420 sections. The details of the laws governing those who might deserve such a verdict are found in the very *last* sections of *Choshen Mishpat*.
>
> Only after one has studied and complied with all the laws from the beginning of *Orach Chaim*, [the first volume] until these concluding ones, may one presume to rule on these regulations.

In other words, if a person behaves cruelly towards a fellow Jew, claiming that the Torah sanctions such behavior, it is possible (aside from perhaps misinterpreting the *halacha*) that he is really motivated by something else. Perhaps his behavior is fueled by his own bad temperament, despite his rationalization that his conduct is prompted by his fear of G-d. In contrast, when a person does a favor for another, there is no doubt whatsoever that a mitzvah has been performed.

---

17. See *Likkutei Sichot* vol. 1, p. 133.

OTHER TITLES IN
THE CHASIDIC HERITAGE SERIES

Yom Tov Shel Rosh Hashanah 5659—Discourse One

Yom Tov Shel Rosh Hashanah 5659—Discourse Two (Coming Soon)

Vayishlach Yehoshua 5736—Garments of the Soul

Studies in Rashi—The Third Party

Mayim Rabbim 5738—The Unbreakable Soul

DEDICATED

IN MEMORY OF OUR PARENTS

**MEIR** BEN **ARIE CHALFON**

&

**RACHEL** BAT **SABATINO FRESCO**

OF BLESSED MEMORY